Guiding Principles for Success:
GPS Map

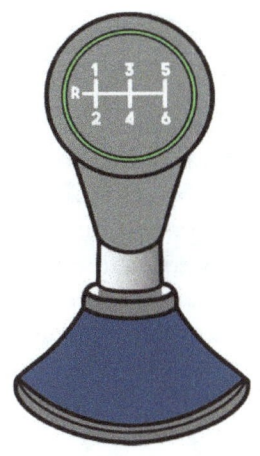

Dr. Lester Frederick

Personal Goals

Paired ⟷ Goals

GPS Toolbox

Preface

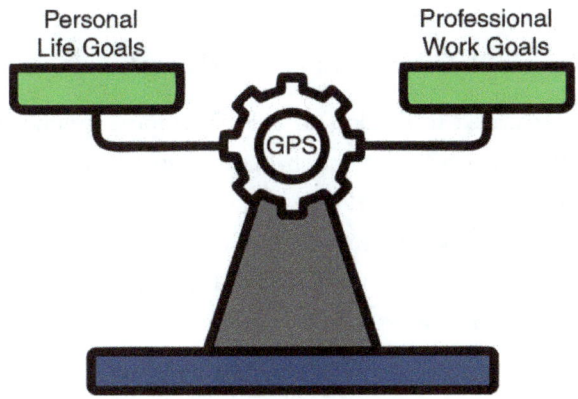

Early Awakening Through Reading and Self-Discovery

I became addicted to reading at seventeen after completing my first full book, a requirement to graduate high school following a failed attempt the year before. Because I didn't believe I was smart enough for college, I chose to start working instead. Around that time, I met a young businessman who introduced me to business and self-help books.

A Search for Identity, Purpose, and Passion

In my twenties, I became deeply interested in guiding principles for life and success, drawn in by books, articles, and speakers. The concepts of purpose and identity had the greatest impact on me, followed closely by passion. Over time, I realized that others had experienced similar moments of illumination, some through spiritual journeys, others through practical experience, and many through a blend of both.

Academic Foundations in Learning, Leadership, and Business

Having earned an MBA with a concentration in leadership and an Ed.D. with a concentration in instructional technology and distance education has helped clarify and communicate these guiding principles.

Synthesizing Professional Experience Across Disciplines and Cultures

Working across various fields, including hospitality, construction, instructional design, and digital project management, has deepened my understanding of core fundamentals such as planning, problem-solving, and profitability. Coupled with insights gained from extensive travel and exposure to multiple cultures, this diverse experience eventually led to my being known as "The Synthesiza," a reflection of my passion for synthesizing knowledge and skills across disciplines.

Twenty-Five Years of Refinement and Breakthrough

Over the years, I struggled to develop an eclectic template grounded in key success principles for both personal and professional goals. Later, I expanded the template to include overlapping frameworks such as mission, vision, and values. After about 25 years of sporadic reflection and experimentation, everything finally clicked into place at the end of 2024! I wish this had happened sooner so I could have applied it more comprehensively over the years, but everything comes in its own time.

Jack Canfield, a multiple *New York Times* bestselling author who interviewed hundreds of people, stated, "The most successful people I know create superior results [such as achieving goals] yet still maintain a balance among work, family, and recreation in their lives."[1] This may be difficult, but it is not impossible, especially if you are satisfied with your view of what represents a realistically successful, balanced life.

From Insight to Action: The Birth of This Book

From late 2024 into 2025, I felt compelled to write this book. Its centerpiece is the refined and synthesized template now called interactive worksheets or interactive infographics. To date, I'm unaware of any other comprehensive, customizable two-page interactive worksheet like this.

Create Your Own Actionable GPS Map

The downloadable interactive worksheets contain six prompts: Personality (Identity), Purpose, Passion, Problem-Solving, Planning, and Profit. You will use these prompts to construct your six Guiding Principles for Success (GPS), which will produce your own GPS Map containing your goals. Your completed GPS Map will function like a treasure map, guiding you on a quest to achieve those goals. Have fun while getting it done. Drive on!

Lester
idldcreatives.com

---

[1] Canfield, *The Success Principles*

Acknowledgement

I'm grateful to God for my mother, whose support has been constant throughout my life.

"Life is one big road with lots of signs ...
don't bury your thoughts.
Put your vision to reality." –Bob Marley

Introduction: Start Your Engine!

"Cultivate balance by achieving goals at work and home."
–Dr. Travis G. Parry

Sometimes, as we try to shift our lives into gear, we feel stuck, hanging between our personal goals and our professional goals, unsure of how to bridge the gap to move forward.

But now, you can create your own high-level **Guiding Principles for Success**, or **GPS**, to help you get from where you are to where you want to be. Your customized GPS Map can help you get your work life or student life on track, and from there, it will continue to guide you on your journey.

So, drop the top, pump up the sound, grab the wheel, feel the breeze, and let's roll!

Defining Success

There are many definitions of success and work-life balance. You probably have your own. In one article on work-life balance, Bulger writes, "Some definitions suggest that work-life balance is the ability to accomplish the goals set in both work and personal life and achieve satisfaction in all life domains. Other definitions suggest that the term 'balance' implies equal engagement in and satisfaction with work and personal life roles."[2]

Within the context of this book, bridging your personal and professional goals is closely related to maintaining a work-life balance (WLB). For many, a healthy work-life balance equates to an enhanced and more successful quality of life.

Therefore, *success is defined as bridging and achieving your personal life goals and professional work goals to create a fairly balanced life.*

Striving for Balance

Creating a professional work–personal life balance is easier said than done. Imagine a bridge stretching across a river, with two distinct shores on either side. One side of the bridge represents your personal goals. These might include family, health, education, hobbies, and personal growth. The other side symbolizes your professional goals, such as career advancement, financial success, and business ambitions.

The roadway of the bridge is the path you take to navigate both worlds. It's where time management, prioritization, and boundaries come into play. By managing how much time, energy, and resources you spend on each side of the bridge, you can ensure that your goals complement each other.

The center of the bridge is where both worlds meet, often symbolizing the area of balance. This is where decisions are made about how, where, and

---

[2] Bulger, "Work-Life Balance."

when to devote your time. Striking a good balance here means actively deciding when to drive forward and when to reverse.

Some days, you might lean more toward personal goals (taking a day off to focus on a family situation); other days, you might focus more toward professional goals (putting in extra hours to close a deal or finish a project). The key is flexibility and knowing when to lean into one side without feeling overwhelmed by the other. Balancing both sides effectively will look different for everybody, and there isn't a perfect formula. "If your work-life balance supports your well-being and goals, then it's effective."[3]

Personal and professional goals don't have to be opposing forces. The bridge helps maintain the connection between them, allowing you to move forward with purpose while preserving balance on both sides. The key is to continuously adjust, ensuring that both sides receive the attention they deserve without driving too far in one direction. Regular check-ins with your GPS Map allow you to stay aligned to ensure that your journey remains fulfilling and meaningful.

---

[3] Taylor, *From Burnout to Balance*.

Your Destination Objective

During this journey of discovery, you will design your own executable GPS Map that will bridge your foundational personal and professional goals for a more balanced life.

"Achieving work-life balance is not a one-time goal to check off, but an ongoing journey."
–Nathan Shaw

Driving Directions

- You're not a passenger. You're a GPS Driver.
- Have an open mind and a receptive heart, even while driving on unfamiliar roads.
- You'll answer questions soon, and you can refine your answers later.
- It's best to complete each chapter in order.
- Success isn't guaranteed, but consistently applying the GPS can be transformative.
- You'll be able to download your editable GPS Map worksheets on another page.
- Remember that the downloadable worksheets are copyrighted and are for your use only.
- There are word count limitations on the downloadable PDFs.
- Use the eBook or print version and the GPS Map together.

Describe, Assemble, and Practice (DAP)

Below are six GPS prompts you will use in assembling your Guiding Principles for Success (GPS).

Six Prompts:

1. Personality (Identity)
2. Purpose
3. Passion
4. Problem-Solving
5. Plan
6. Profit

Together, we will DAP each of these GPS prompts.

1. **Describe** by explaining and understanding each GPS prompt.
2. **Assemble** by creating your customized GPS.
3. **Practice** by test-driving each GPS.

Guiding is like having your hands on the steering wheel, helping you navigate using directions.

Principles represent six roads with signs and guardrails that keep you safe and focused.

Success is using your GPS Map to bridge and achieve your goals in a way that creates a more balanced life.

Personal Goals Introduction

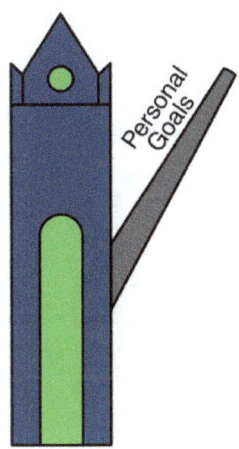

Your Personal Goals are on one side of the work-life bridge. Your three prompts to create your personal Guiding Principles for Success are:

- Personality (Identity)
- Purpose
- Passion

Laying this foundation first can rev up your engine and get you moving on the road to a successful life. Remember, a "successful life" is one that is fairly balanced between work accomplishments and personal pursuits.

Once you have a clear understanding, or confirmation, of your personality (identity), it becomes easier to define your purpose and align it with your passion.

Purpose acts as a compass, guiding you through moments of doubt or uncertainty. It connects your actions to something greater than yourself and infuses each task with significance.

Passion, on the other hand, is the fuel that propels you forward, making the process of achieving your goals exciting and energizing.

Chapter 1: Personality (Identity)

"Know who you are. Accept who you are. Be who you are."
–Anonymous

Description: Who Do You Think You Are?

What kind of car would you be if you could transform into one? Each car has a unique vehicle identification number, or VIN, just like you have a unique fingerprint that identifies you.

You should begin with Who you are (Personality/Identity) in order to know Why you're here (Purpose).

Identity is who you *are*. It is not what you *do*. Some people have adopted identities based on what is shared on social media, but you should not allow social media to define you.

If you ask most people who they are, they will probably answer with what they do. For example: "I'm a teacher." In reality, you're a person (that's who you *are*) who teaches (that's what you *do*).

That's not just a simple play on words or semantics. That's why people sometimes say they need to take a trip to "find themselves." While travel can help, no matter where you go, you are still you. However, some people spend so long fulfilling a role that they need uninterrupted time to remember who they truly are or to discover themselves without outside influence.

Identity and personality are connected, but they're not the same. "Your personality is the outward expression of your inner identity" is a pertinent statement attributed to Carl Jung. Personality can change due to aging or different situations. However, some believe that identity is primarily tied to unchanging factors such as nationality, ethnicity, race, biological parents, family lineage, or birth order. Even if someone is adopted or unaware of their biological parents, they can still discover their identity and find assurance in it.

There are different types of identities: personal, social, group, occupational, and online. This chapter focuses on personal identity.

"Personal identity concerns self-sameness and continuity of perceptions of who one is across multiple domains or aspects in life."[4]

Identity is not about titles, degrees, status, political affiliation, fashion, money, followers, likes, your favorite team, or anything that you can achieve, buy, or choose to add to your name. Within reason, nothing is wrong with those things, but identity is found under the hood. It's not in the accessories like fancy wheels or an all-leather interior.

---

[4] Branje, de Moor, Spitzer, and Becht. "Dynamics of Identity Development in Adolescence."

Who are you minus what you do and what you have? Pause to let that download into your soul. It's an important question to ponder. The answer to it might tell you who you really are. Answers might include your age/generation, gender, spirituality, culture, etc.

You are a one-of-a-kind human be-ing, not a human do-ing. Therefore, you shouldn't compare yourself with others but instead be comfortable in your own skin as a unique person. That includes accepting yourself with your flaws, because everybody has flaws. "Imperfections are not inadequacies; they are reminders that we're all in this together."[5]

Do You Know Who You Are?

The proclamation "Know Thyself" has been repeated throughout recorded history for centuries. In the film *42*,[6] Chadwick Boseman portrays Jackie Robinson. Robinson faced a lot of opposition as a major league baseball player, and that is depicted in the film. After many frustrating experiences, Boseman (as Robinson) confidently states: "I know who I am."

In the animated film *The Lion King*, Mufasa says to his son Simba: "Remember who you are." But in order to *remember* who you are, you must first *know* who you are.

Unfortunately, some excessive social media algorithms can practically program you to think, feel, and do contrary to your true identity.

"The multiplicity of digital identities that individuals maintain across different platforms can lead to a more complex and fragmented sense of self ... This phenomenon underscores the dynamic and multifaceted nature of digital identity and its significant impact on self-identity construction in the digital age."[7]

---

[5] Brown, *Gifts of Imperfection.*
[6] Directed by Brian Helgeland, 2013.
[7] Rosana and Fauzi, "Role of Digital Identity."

The conscious hip-hop trio De La Soul, whose name means "of the soul," had a hit single in 1989 titled "Me, Myself, and I." In the music video, they are shown being ridiculed and bullied to conform to societal norms. They resist the pressure and visually display that "Me, Myself, I" means to stay true to oneself even if it's unpopular to do so. That's a "clutch move." In a car, a clutch helps safely shift gears and speeds; therefore, a clutch move is a timely and decisive action that shifts you forward. Maybe you've seen characters in *The Fast and the Furious* movies push down the clutch with their feet and shift gears with their hands in the proper sequence. Precision and coordination are critical. Your clutch moves might not look as cool, but it's the results that matter. Make your clutch moves—like a GPS Driver—to propel forward and level up!

The song is not about isolating yourself. The song promotes personal identity and personality by encouraging listeners to embrace who they are, without relying on external validation or trying to be someone they're not. You can't please everyone, and there'll always be haters. So, brush them off like flies. Or, turn their negativity into your source of motivation. Remember, some may attempt to make you feel inferior due to their own insecurities. They might label you with terms like "dumb," "nerd," "weirdo," "geek," "fat," and "ugly" or use various gendered, ethnic, and racial slurs. Instead of mirroring their behaviors, remember our common humanity and embrace the humor of comedians like Fluffy, who jokes: "Me racist? The only race I hate is the one you have to run."[8]

Identity Theft

The worst form of identity theft happens when society hacks your identity, causing you to believe and behave in ways that aren't true to who you really are. An identity crisis can be stressful, but sometimes it can lead to beneficial self-discovery. It seems like sometimes, an identity crisis can help

---

[8] Iglesias, *I'm Not Fat ... I'm Fluffy.*

people discover their identity, be transformed into who they were supposed to be, or both. It's like a dusty caterpillar crawling into a dark cocoon and eventually flying out as an attractive butterfly. The biological term is metamorphosis, which refers to a transformation. It's a major enhancement that should be celebrated. However, it's amazing how even people who are close to you might say something like, 'You've changed,' with a negative connotation. Well, yes, and one shouldn't want to become a caterpillar again.

Knowing who you are and being true to yourself can provide stability in this ever-changing world regardless of your age. Branje et al.[9] state, "Adolescents who have firm identity commitments steadily report better psychosocial adjustments over time compared to those who continue to experience identity ambiguity." Truly knowing yourself can provide a sense of identity within community because sometimes you have to stand with others, and sometimes you have to stand alone.

According to George,[10] human beings have a body, a soul, and a spirit, and part of our identity includes our gender. There are different schools of thought on this, but being confident in and accepting of your gender, along with the other dimensions of yourself, is essential to achieving a sense of wholeness and well-being.

Shania Twain on Identity

It seems that Shania Twain, the country pop queen, initially struggled with her identity as a woman and with her body image. Eventually, it appears that she discovered and embraced her identity.

Shania's real name is Eilleen Regina Edwards. She adopted the stage name "Shania" as a teenager; it is derived from an Ojibwe word meaning "I'm on my way." The Ojibwe are one of the largest Native American tribes in the

---

[9] "Dynamics of Identity Development."
[10] *Classic Christianity.*

northern United States and Canada. Twain said, "I haven't personally investigated the Edwards family genealogy myself, but my understanding of what my mother explained is that they had a mixed background of French-Canadian and Native Indian."[11] In addition, the surname Edwards is common in England, so it's possible that her family were of British descent.

Born in Windsor, Ontario, in 1965, Shania grew up in extreme poverty in a small, rundown house. As a child, she would do a lot of roleplaying. Many times, she wondered if she should be an actress, since she so enjoyed acting like someone other than herself. To help support the family, her mother, Sharon Morrison, would take young Shania, to perform her musical talents in local bars. "I spent my whole youth hiding behind a tomboy image, trying to hide my figure," she said later.[12]

In a 2025 interview, Shania opened up about her longstanding insecurities regarding her body, sharing that she had experienced numerous unwanted and inappropriate touches while growing up. She said "I was in abusive situations where you hate being a woman. I hated being a girl."[13] Once, when her mother asked about her ambitions, she said she wanted to be a bodybuilder, a tough man whom no one would dare mess with.

Tragedy struck when Shania was twenty-two. Both of her parents were killed in a car crash, and she was suddenly thrust into the role of caregiver for her three younger siblings.

Her journey in Nashville was filled with rejection as she struggled to make it in the competitive music industry. With a rural background and unpolished communication skills, she often felt out of place.

Her first husband was Robert John "Mutt" Lange, a renowned music producer. Mutt helped to craft Shania's distinctive blend of country and

---

[11] Twain, *From This Moment On*.
[12] Eggar, *Shania Twain*, 59.
[13] Garibaldi and Harkin, "Shania Twain."

pop. The first hit album they made together was *The Woman in Me*, released in 1995. That album achieved multi-platinum status and helped redefine the sound of country music. Despite their massive success, Shania and her husband were not considered "authentic" country figures by some influential people.

As she became more popular, many questioned the accuracy of her lineage and identity. Eventually, Shania addressed their concerns. Around the time Shania was two years old, her mother and father, Clarence Edwards, parted ways. Shortly after, Jerry Twain stepped into the role of being her father. A few years later, Shania's mother married Jerry, and he legally adopted Shania and her siblings. While Shania is unsure of the exact amount of Native American ancestry she has, she was legally recognized as 50 percent Native American after being adopted by Jerry who is a full-blooded Native American.

In 2003, she was diagnosed with Lyme disease. The illness, contracted from a tick bite, caused severe symptoms including chronic fatigue. Most notably, it led to her losing her voice, a devastating blow that threatened both her career and her passion for music. For years, Twain struggled with vocal problems, and doctors, initially, failed to diagnose the cause. It wasn't until 2008 that the connection between her vocal issues and Lyme disease was fully understood. Twain eventually underwent multiple surgeries and intense vocal therapy.

In 2008, Shania discovered that her best friend had had an affair with her husband. In 2010, Shania got a divorce. Then, her former best friend married her ex-husband. That caused immense emotional pain and deep feelings of betrayal.

During a 2011 interview, Shania mentioned that she might have been detached from life over the years. Maybe she had to compartmentalize her life experiences as a coping mechanism for the trauma and challenges she faced. Even during her rise to fame, she maintained a fairly private persona.

By acknowledging this detachment, she began the process of reuniting with her true self and sharing her journey in her memoir *From This Moment On*. Shania said, "So, I've reconnected and said, no, this is actually who I am. I'm neither embarrassed of who I am, where I come from, what I've experienced."[14]

Years later, in 2017, after a lot of therapy and vocal training, Shania regained her singing voice and released the album *Now*. The album marked her first studio release in fifteen years and reflects her personal growth, resilience, and journey through heartbreak and healing.

During a 2025 interview, Shania recalled a moment when she was behind the camera, looking at herself, and was pleasantly surprised by who and what she saw. Shania said, "I was like, wow, I'm actually a woman after all, and I think I might like it. When I wrote 'Man! I Feel Like a Woman!' it was an absolute celebration [of that]."[15]

The song was conceived in 1994 when she co-wrote it with her then-husband and producer, "Mutt." It was released on her album Come On Over in 1997, and the music video followed in 1999. Over the years, it seems that Shania gradually reclaimed her identity as a woman, or perhaps discovered part of her identity, and began to embrace her body as it is. This turning point marked a deeper self-acceptance and celebration of herself.

Combat Veterans and Identity

Disclaimer: This section addresses challenges faced by military veterans, particularly combat veterans. Feedback was received from veterans to ensure respectful representation. There are signs that many military veterans, particularly combat veterans, face difficulties in affirming their core identity, especially when transitioning back into civilian life. This is why it's important for those who have never served in the military to

---

[14] ABC News, "Shania Twain."
[15] Garibaldi and Harkin, "Shania Twain."

recognize and respect the sacrifices they have made, giving so much of themselves to ensure our safety and freedom. Dr. Jonathan Shay was a clinical psychiatrist at the Department of Veteran Affairs Outpatient Clinic who attended to Vietnam veterans suffering from combat trauma. In his book *Achilles in Vietnam*, Shay focuses on veterans' experiences upon returning from war and on promoting the mental and physical safety of soldiers.

Shay's book has actual details from therapy sessions (with permission from the veterans). "When a survivor of prolonged trauma loses all sense of meaningful personal narrative, this may result in a contaminated identity."[16]

One Vietnam veteran shared that he had a good upbringing, but when he reflected on the contrast between how he was raised and the things he did as a soldier, he was horrified. He repeatedly spoke about the evil he witnessed and experienced during the war. The veteran said, "I just look at it like it was somebody else. I really do. It was somebody else."[17]

Some described themselves as having behaved like animals, later overwhelmed by pain and regret once their frenzied state, known as berserking, had passed. "Berserking" refers to a state of intense, uncontrollable rage or frenzy, often associated with the Viking warriors known as berserkers. These warriors were believed to enter a trance-like battle frenzy during which they exhibited extraordinary strength and aggression.

It may seem unnatural or incomprehensible to some that a person could exist in such a state to the point that individual doesn't associate his true self with the person he was during combat. However, in an active combat situation, a person must be fully committed to the mission, his leadership, and his team to have the best chance of seeing members return home safely.

---

[16] Shay, *Achilles in Vietnam*.
[17] Shay.

Emotional detachment protects him from overthinking or irrational decisions while the frenzied state protects him with an adrenaline boost that may help his courage, physical ability, and resolve to complete the mission. The challenge of adjusting to life outside of battle-ready mode areas awaits when they return.

Some of the same behaviors and feelings are demonstrated in the soldiers in the 2010 documentary *Restrepo*. In it, Sergeant Brendon O'Bryne says, "I've built my lifestyle for the last twelve months here getting shot at, you know? So, I'm just going to take time to work that out, you know? And then it's going to take a while for me to get 'un-oo-rah,' if you know what I'm saying."[18]

It's clear that Sergeant O'Bryne wisely knows that he acts differently during military combat than in the civilian world, and that adjusting takes time. "Oo-rah" is a motivational exclamation used primarily by the United States Marine Corps to express enthusiasm, determination, and camaraderie. It's a battle cry that boosts morale during training or combat, as are the other branches' phrases like "hoo-ah" in the Army and "hoo-yah" in the Navy and Coast Guard.

Restrepo was directed by Tim Hetherington and Sebastian Junger. It focuses on the lives of US soldiers deployed to the Restrepo outpost in Afghanistan during the war in the Korengal Valley, one of the most dangerous postings in the US military at the time. The documentary captures the day-to-day realities of combat and shows the soldiers' interactions with each other, including their moments of fear, humor, and camaraderie as well as their struggles with the harsh conditions of war.

The documentary's approach is highly immersive, with the filmmakers embedding themselves with the soldiers and gaining unprecedented access to their lives both on and off the battlefield. One of the central themes of

---

[18] *Restrepo*, directed by Tim Hetherington and Sebastian Junger.

Restrepo is the bond formed between the soldiers as they face life-threatening situations together. The film also explores the trauma of war and includes moments of profound loss and grief, particularly after the death of soldier Juan "Doc" Restrepo, for whom the outpost was named.

Combat Veterans: From Active Duty to Civilian Life

Christine Haines sheds more light on the identity of combat veterans in a 2024 dissertation titled *Experience of Transition from Active Duty to Civilian Life for Post 9/11 Combat Veterans*. This study explores the deeply personal and psychological challenges faced by veterans when they leave the structured, mission-driven life of the military.

The study had some limitations; the sample size was only nine participants and all were male. Regardless, the results provided broader implications about the concern of associating one's identity with *doing* rather than with *being*.

This distinction is especially important in the context of military service, where one's worth is often measured by performance, rank, or role. Everyone is naturally born a human being. Therefore, nothing can be added to or taken away from our identity as human beings. This simple truth can sometimes challenge the performance-based identity that many veterans adopt during their service. The data from the study offers powerful insights into how one's identity can be fragmented and reconstructed post-service.

After leaving active duty, many veterans expect their military skills to carry over into civilian life. However, they often encounter obstacles when trying to apply those skills outside the military. This is a common struggle: a mismatch between perceived value in one environment versus another. The skills that gave veterans confidence and purpose in the military often don't find the same recognition in civilian careers, which contributes to identity confusion. Veterans often feel disoriented when the military structure, where roles, ranks, and responsibilities define identity, is suddenly removed. Civilian life can lack the clarity and purpose that military roles once provided. A disconnect occurs when those titles no longer apply, leaving veterans to reconstruct a sense of self without familiar validation. This can be particularly jarring in a society that may not fully grasp or appreciate military culture. Returning to a former version of one's life can feel like regression, amplifying feelings of failure and confusion.

Most of the participants indicated they "experienced a crisis of identity after confronting barriers in the civilian world. This crisis of identity caused them to ask, 'Who am I?' and/or 'What do I do?'"[19] Dr. Janna Koretz, as one of the authors of *Boundaries, Priorities, and Finding Work-Life Balance*, said "While identifying closely with your career isn't necessarily bad, it makes you vulnerable to a painful identity crisis if you burn out, get laid off, or retire."[20]

Many people equate what they *do*, which is about positions and performance, with who they *are*, which is about identity. That can cause confusion, because eventually you'll have to ask: Who are you when you're not doing anything, like working? This dilemma doesn't affect only veterans; it's a universal human challenge. Understanding the difference between *intrinsic identity* and *external role* can be a key part of post-transition healing and reintegration. How we view ourselves can influence how we act. For example, after failing at something important, a person might start to see themselves as a failure, which can cause them to think and behave as if they're insignificant and defeated. We think, we feel, we decide, and we act. That said, viewing yourself as a billionaire king or queen does not automatically make it true, but the way you see yourself can still affect your behavior.

All veterans adopted different ways of coping with identity challenges during their transition, using both constructive and harmful strategies at

---

[19] Haines, "Experience of Transition," 27.
[20] Harvard Business Review, *Boundaries, Priorities, and Finding Work-Life Balance.*

various stages of the process. This variation highlights the fact that healing is not linear; veterans may switch between productive and destructive strategies as they try to regain footing.

Some of the negative coping mechanisms were excessive drinking, drugs, isolation, antisocial behavior, and suicidal ideation. These destructive responses often stem from a lack of direction, support, or a sense of purpose, and reflect the intensity of emotional pain that veterans may carry.

Some of the positive coping mechanisms explored in the Haines study were reflection, reaching out, engaging in treatment programs, and spirituality. These approaches, while not always immediate or easy to access, offer hope for long-term healing.

One veteran recounted how it felt to receive helpful assistance at the right time, saying, "When I was feeling pissed off and wanted to kill myself and go do risky behavior, they told me before I do anything to write a poem ... next thing I know, I didn't want to kill myself anymore."[21] This powerful moment illustrates how creative expression and human connection can act as lifelines in moments of crisis, providing breakthroughs. For some, choosing to be spiritually grounded can offer a renewed sense of meaning and identity beyond military achievements. That's a clutch move!

Naturally, people hold varying beliefs about the components that make up a human being. Remember the importance of keeping an open mind and a receptive heart, even when you encounter viewpoints that differ from your own. Otherwise, it's easy to develop blind spots and miss key landmarks along your journey. For example, some people believe in spirituality or God and others don't. That's their choice, and we shouldn't judge others with a pointed finger. According to George,[22] we are primarily spiritual beings. Figure 1.1 illustrates that human beings consist of a spirit, soul, and body, which together form the foundation of our identity. The body is like a solid

---

[21] Haines, 42.

[22] *Classic Christianity.*

block of ice, the soul like water as it melts, and the spirit like vapor when the water is heated. Each is distinct, yet all are part of the same essence.

Figure 1.1. Personality (Identity) Chart

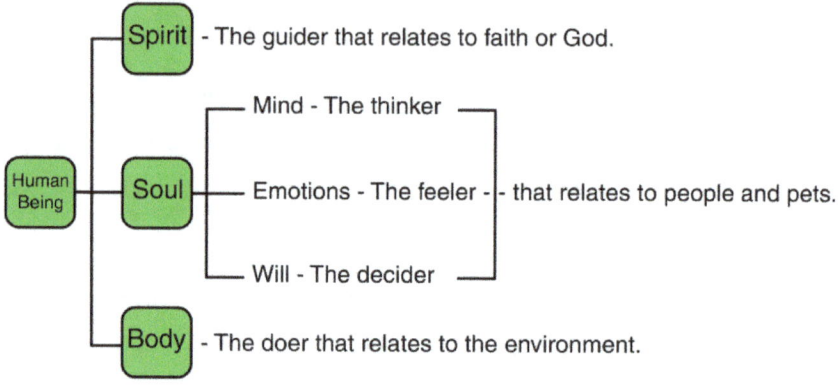

"You are not just a body with a soul; you are primarily a spiritual being."
–Bob George

The Many Dimensions of Identity and Personality

Identity and Personality are multidimensional. Genealogy tools such as DNA testing services can be helpful in understanding your identity because they can provide insights into your genetic background, ethnic origins, family tree, and cultural roots. Researching your history may help answer questions, such as why you feel drawn to certain fields, activities, or locations. You may discover that many connected to you did those things as well. Think about a time you've talked with a friend and realized that most of their family found their way into the same field: medicine, education, journalism, athletics, etc.

For example, in one episode of PBS's Finding Your Roots, actor John Lithgow was shocked when he saw his extended family tree included actors Clint Eastwood and Sally Fields. In another episode, he discovered that the show's host, Dr. Henry Louis Gates Jr., was his cousin.[23]

Although they aren't perfect, there are also assessments you can take to help you determine your own personality type. One such assessment is the Myers-Briggs Type Indicator (MBTI). It's an assessment, not a "test" because there are no right or wrong personalities. We are all unique individuals.

The MBTI asks you questions to discover your personality type. The assessment simply considers whether you tend to be introverted or extroverted and whether you gather information directly through your five senses of sight, sound, smell, taste and touch or indirectly through your "gut." It also looks at how you draw conclusions using logic or emotion and whether you live cautiously by following rules or more spontaneously by taking things as they come.

Discovering your MBTI personality type can help you to understand yourself a little more clearly. One personality isn't better than another; all of them have strengths and weaknesses of various types. But the better you know yourself, the better you can learn to reinforce your strengths and improve upon your weaknesses.

When you understand your personality type, you will gain insight into how you naturally approach decision-making, problem-solving, and interacting with others. This awareness allows you to make choices that are better informed, and these choices ultimately lead to greater fulfillment and effectiveness in various areas of your life. Once confirmed, stand firm and don't compromise your identity.

---

[23] Ancestry, "John Lithgow."

Instructions:
Look in the Past Through the Rearview Mirror

Download your editable GPS Map worksheets via the QR code below, or by entering gpsmap.idldcreatives.com into your browser.

Use your phone's camera to scan the QR code.
Then select the link that appears.

Now, it's time to create your own Personality (Identity) GPS with the GPS Map worksheet that you downloaded. You can also input text in the physical book. It's critical to know your history in order to know your destiny. You'll create your core guiding personality (identity) principle by using as many identity factors as you like, such as your full name, race, ethnicity, nationality, gender, and spirituality. Your name can include your maiden name. Some of this will be found on your identification card (e.g., your driver's license). Try your best to input only one brief sentence for each question. That will keep your answers focused and memorable.

Do not add titles or positions, such as "manager" or "artist." Those titles are about what you do, not who you are. Remember, it's important to respect each person's individuality, especially in group settings, even if we disagree. Following is a general example. Feel free to describe yourself in your own words.

Example

Who are you? (Identity)

I am John Doe an Asian American man who believes in God.

Where are you from? (History)

I was born in the USA, and my parents have roots in Korea.

Combine both answers into one sentence (preferably)

I am John Doe, an Asian American man born in the USA with family roots in Korea, and I believe in God.

Assemble

Fill in the blanks in the GPS Map with one brief sentence each.

Who are you? (Identity)

I am _____

_____

Where are you from? (History)

I am from _____

_____

Combine both answers into one sentence (preferably)

_____

_____

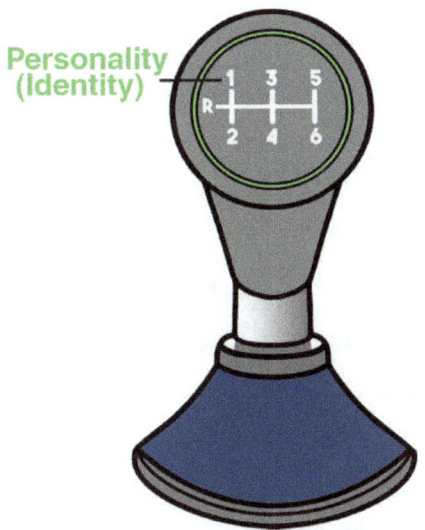

Practice: Reinforce Your Personality (Identity) GPS

Shift: Symbolically shift into the Personality GPS first gear. Yes, you can make a verbal engine sound effect and simulate the motion by physically shifting your hand, similar to how some people 'air drum.'

Reinforce: For example, you can replace negative thinking with thoughts of being a person of worth and significance. Memorize your Personality (Identity) GPS.

Describe and/or draw your own ways of practicing your Personality (Identity) GPS.

_____

_____

_____

_____

_____

_____

_____

_____

Chapter 2: Purpose

"Without purpose, life is motion without meaning."
–Rick Warren

Description: Why Are You Here?

A car's purpose is to be driven, but what's your purpose as a human being? Purpose is the driving force behind our actions; it is the "why" that propels us forward.

Purpose in action is like your hands on the steering wheel, adjusting the vehicle's course with the directions from your car or phone's GPS to get you where you want to go. Your purpose is your reason for existing and living. It answers the questions "Why are you here?" "Why do you do what you do?" and "Where are you going?" These questions are important because knowing why you're here (Purpose) and where you are (Reality) can help you determine where you want to go (Destiny). Living without a clear purpose can be like being stuck in the mud and spinning your wheels. You're moving but not making forward progress.

Life can be like driving in the *Gran Turismo* or *Mario Kart* game: Sometimes, you'll spin out of control and go off track. But you have to get back on course. You're not just driving aimlessly; you are on the tracks of life for a cause. Every turn, boost, or setback is part of the trip.

"Research shows that combining the elements you have defined as 'you' in a way that aligns with your purpose will make you happier, more psychologically healthy, and better able to achieve your goals and ambitions."[24]

In the journey of life, many of us yearn to find a deeper sense of meaning, a calling that resonates with who we truly are. This calling isn't just about a job or a role in society; it's a profound alignment with what we were uniquely designed to do.

Sometimes, well-meaning but misguided traditions, superstitions, and religious practices can lead us to a dead end rather than toward our true purpose. Some people equate purpose with their life's calling. While those two things may not be entirely the same, they are intimately connected. Discovering your purpose generates direction, significance, confidence, respect, and a sense of belonging. When we live out our calling, we both enrich our own lives and positively affect the lives of those around us. Otherwise, we might end up wasting time with excessive day dreaming, doom scrolling, and binge watching.

The band U2 seems to be singing about the universal longing to know the purpose of life in their song "I Still Haven't Found What I'm Looking For." The lead singer tells us of the travels he's made to find answers, his high and

---

[24] Murden, *Defining You.*

low moments, and even his beliefs about life overall. The message, wrapped in the title, seems to be that he needs to know there's something beyond merely existing.

This resonates with the human experience of searching for deeper meaning in life. Sometimes, beneath the surface of success, relationships, and achievement, many people still feel a quiet yearning, a sense that something essential is missing. The song captures that restless ache, the soul's desire for fulfillment that goes beyond material or temporary satisfaction. It's a reminder that the journey toward purpose is often filled with questions, detours, and moments of doubt. Yet in that searching, there is also hope, a belief that what we're looking for is real, even if we haven't found it yet.

Michael Phelps is the world's most decorated Olympian. However, even with more than a dozen gold medals to his name, he still felt like something was missing. Eventually, he was able to say, "Reading *A Purpose Driven Life* changed my perspective on life and helped me find my purpose."[25]

There are some similarities with discovering our purpose and the "hero's journey," a storytelling framework that outlines a common narrative pattern found in myths, books, and movies, popularized by Joseph Campbell in his book *The Hero with a Thousand Faces*. It's a way to show growth and transformation through challenges. Films such as *Star Wars* (original trilogy), *The Lord of the Rings*, *The Lion King*, and *The Matrix*, along with books like *The Odyssey*, *The Alchemist*, and *The Hobbit*, all follow the classic hero's journey framework. Figure 2.1 illustrates the stages of the Hero's Journey and their relation to discovering one's purpose

---

[25] Phelps and Abrahamson, *No Limits*.

Figure 2.1. The Hero's Journey in Relation to Discovering One's Purpose

Stages of the Hero's Journey	Relation to Discovering One's Purpose
1. Ordinary World	Feeling that something is missing
2. Call to Adventure	Realizing life can have a deeper meaning
3. Refusal of the Call	Fearing change and resisting the journey toward purpose
4. Meeting the Mentor	Receiving guidance from others who offer advice and resources
5. Crossing the Threshold	Stepping into the unknown in pursuit of purpose and growth
6. Tests, Allies, and Enemies	Facing challenges that refine and shape one's calling
7. Approach to the Inmost Cave	Engaging in deep reflection to confront inner fears and doubts
8. The Ordeal	Undergoing a transformational crisis that clarifies true purpose
9. The Reward	Gaining insight into true reason for living in this world
10. The Road Back	Returning with purpose aligned to identity and daily life
11. The Resurrection	Embodying purpose after a final test and transformation
12. Return with the Elixir	Inspiring others to discover their own purpose

Ikigai

The Japanese term *ikigai*, which is loosely interpreted as "having a fulfilling life," promotes what Héctor García and Francesc Miralles called "a harmonious relationship between personal passions and professional goals."

Ikigai embodies the idea that life is most fulfilling when we live with a sense of purpose that integrates our passions, talents, values, and contributions to the world. This concept isn't just philosophical. It is lived out in the daily rhythms and attitudes of many people in Japan, especially in the region of Okinawa. "According to those born in Okinawa, the island with the most centenarians in the world, our ikigai is the reason we get up in the morning."[26]

In this community, where people live notably long and healthy lives, ikigai is more than an abstract notion. It is deeply woven into their culture and lifestyle. Their ikigai may come from nurturing their gardens, caring for loved ones, practicing crafts, or contributing to their local community in meaningful ways. "Research clearly indicates that the Okinawans' focus on ikigai gives a sense of purpose to each and every day and plays an important role in their health and longevity."[27]

---

[26] García and Miralles, *Ikigai*.
[27] García and Miralles.

This sense of purpose motivates Okinawans to live actively. It also fosters emotional resilience, social connection, and a positive outlook, all of which are key factors in living a long and satisfying life. In a world often driven by stress and distraction, the Okinawan model of ikigai offers a refreshing reminder that purpose can be simple, grounded, and incredibly powerful.

Most likely, every person has both a general purpose and a specific purpose. For example, the general purpose of a vehicle is to provide transportation. However, the specific purpose of a recreational vehicle or camper van is to allow long-term travel and provide sleeping arrangements.

Your purpose might not be clear now, but it can be revealed over time. It's like seeing a picture of a place that you want to visit in the future. It only becomes clearer when you actually start driving and get closer to that location; finally, the fog is lifted. Then you recognize the real skyline and landscape from the picture.

Purpose Portrayed in Movies

In the animated movie *Soul*, the character Joe Gardner is a jazz musician and music teacher. The movie doesn't clearly explain what purpose is, but it does imply that many people are on the same winding journey of trying to discover their purpose. At one point, Gardner enthusiastically says: "My only purpose on this planet is to play."[28]

Gardner concludes that appreciating and enjoying the little things in everyday living might be his general purpose. From that, we can gather that his specific purpose is to play music. A specific purpose may be tied to a certain person, assignment, time, or something else while a general purpose is the umbrella. Searching for one's purpose in life is like using an actual Global Positioning System (GPS). It keeps recalibrating until you are on the right path.

---

[28] *Soul*, directed by Pete Docter and Kemp Powers.

Freedom Writers, a movie based on a true story, depicts the events that unfold after Erin Gruwell starts her first year of teaching freshman English at an inner-city high school.

As Gruwell finds herself working with a diverse group of at-risk students, the movie conveys lessons about discovering and living out one's purpose. The students in the film come from various challenging backgrounds, and their sense of purpose is often clouded by external struggles like gang violence, poverty, and prejudice.

Gruwell helps some of her students break free from the constraints of their environment. She teaches them that their purpose lies beyond the negativity they've been taught to accept. The act of writing in journals becomes a transformative experience for the students, as it allows them to express themselves, confront the past, and begin to envision a future where they can live out their potential.

Gruwell's own journey demonstrates the importance of perseverance and dedication when it comes to living out one's purpose. Even when faced with resistance, doubt, and lack of support, she remained committed to her students and to the cause.

Scott Glenn portrays Erin's father, Steve Gruwell, in the movie. She thought about going to law school, but explained to her father that in her view, trying to help someone in court meant it was already too late. She believed the real impact needed to happen earlier, in the classroom where change could truly begin.

It seems that Gruwell applied a quotation that is often (though uncertainly) attributed to Benjamin Franklin: "Justice will not be served until those who are unaffected are as outraged as those who are." That reflects Gruwell's mission to express empathy and action among her students, many of whom feel ignored by the broader society.

Maria Reyes, the real-life inspiration for the character Eva Benitez, became involved in gang activities at the age of 11, following in the footsteps of her father and grandfather. By the time she reached high school, she had already witnessed the tragic deaths of over 20 friends due to gang violence. In the film, April Hernandez Castillo portrays the character Eva Benitez, who expresses frustration with Gruwell. Eva questions Gruwell's understanding of the struggles and pain students face, pointing out that Gruwell has no real grasp of their lives or the challenges they deal with outside the classroom. She criticizes the focus on grammar lessons, questioning how it could possibly make a meaningful difference to her life when they were forced to return to their difficult realities. Despite ongoing challenges from many directions, Gruwell enjoys what she is doing. With tears in her eyes, Gruwell tells her husband, Scott Casey, played by actor Patrick Dempsey: "I finally realized what I'm supposed to be doing and I love it. When I'm helping these kids make sense of their lives, everything about my life makes sense to me. How often does a person get that?"[29]

Some of these students were the first in their families to graduate from high school. Some continued their education by going to college. A book version of this story, *The Freedom Writers Diary*, was published in 1999. After graduating from high school, Maria pursued further education at California State University, Long Beach. She later became actively involved with the Freedom Writers Foundation, an organization dedicated to empowering young people through education and writing. Maria has traveled across the country, sharing her personal story and advocating for at-risk youth. Those are clutch moves.

Imagine the countless dedicated educators, especially public school teachers like Erin Gruwell, who have profoundly impacted their students' lives. These are the teachers who often spend extra time and their own

---

[29] *Freedom Writers*, directed by Richard LaGravenese.

money on resources without complaining to create a meaningful learning experience. Don't they deserve more support?

Roleplaying Your Purpose with The Sims

The Sims is a popular series of simulation video games created by Will Wright. Wright's inspiration to create the game came after his house and belongings were burnt to the ground in the 1991 Oakland fires in California. He wanted to simulate rebuilding his life since he had lost so much to the fire. He pitched the game idea to the executives at Maxis, but everybody hated it. Eventually, Electronic Arts purchased Maxis and told Wright to change the game from an electronic dollhouse to *The Sims* as we know it today.[30] Over the years, *The Sims* has become one of the most popular and profitable video games in history. It celebrated its 25th year anniversary in 2025.

You experience the game by building simulated homes, neighborhoods, and even entire cities for the simulated characters that you also create.

This type of game is sometimes called a "sandbox." Players become involved with it for the experience and satisfaction of building their own worlds, rather than simply winning or losing.

Games like *The Sims* offer players unique ways to explore meaning and dig deeper into their own purpose in life. The game allows them to shape the lives, relationships, and aspirations of their virtual characters. By experimenting with different paths, goals, and life choices, players are encouraged to think about what they themselves want to achieve and how they define fulfillment.

The game's feedback system encourages players to consider how they balance their own work-life dynamics, as well as to learn what truly brings them joy.

---

[30] D'Alessandro et al., "The Sims."

Men and Their Purpose

John Eldredge, the author of *Wild at Heart*, believes that modern culture, among other factors, has robbed some men of their adventurous spirit and true purpose. He writes, "You see, it's not just that a man needs a battle to fight; he needs someone to fight for." That "someone" or "something" gives a man a deeper reason to engage with life. Some of these men are rebels, knowingly or unknowingly, seeking a meaningful cause to fight for. Eldredge argues that most men wrestle with a central question: "Do I have what it takes? ... Until a man knows he's a man, he will forever be trying to prove he is one, while at the same time shrinking from anything that might reveal he is not."[31] While views on masculinity vary, competence, significance, and respect are especially important to men.

Scott Galloway is an entrepreneur, author, professor, and father. In one of his 2024 podcasts, Galloway observes,

> There's a growing body of evidence that men are falling behind ... and it's not just a problem for men, it's a problem for women and for our culture, and our politics. The fact is, we have an alarming number of young, lonely, broke men ... who feel as if they have nothing to lose because they have no economic or romantic opportunities. [32]

His remarks highlight the broader social impact of some men feeling adrift and disconnected from meaningful roles and goals. This sense of disconnection can lead some men down a spiraling rabbit hole, where algorithmic disinformation is amplified within echo chambers. It's in these spaces that influential pretenders seek to divide, conquer, monetize, and program us to salivate like Pavlov's research dog.

---

[31] Eldredge, *Wild at Heart: Discovering the Secret of a Man's Soul.*
[32] Galloway and Illing, "Are Men Okay?" *The Prof G Pod with Scott Galloway*, podcast.

Conversely, there are often overlooked real-life examples of productive men stomping forward and leaving lasting footprints for others to follow on the path of growth. Those are clutch moves by GPS Drivers.

Such men, whom I'll call the Breakthrough Bros, avoid unnecessary extremes, knowing how to balance toughness with tenderness. Firm but fair, they understand how to agree to disagree. These productive men do no harm but take no crap. Loving and protecting their families and true friends comes naturally. They accept responsibility rather than shifting blame or resorting to situational ethics. Objective, verifiable facts are relied upon—not unsubstantiated AI hallucinations. Conflict resolution is handled maturely, without vindictiveness.

They understand that the struggle is more about right versus wrong than left versus right, because good and bad exist on all sides. These critical thinking men recognize that *"truth without love is brutality, and love without truth is hypocrisy."* [33] And if they get in trouble, it's good trouble. John Lewis, a steadfast advocate of the rule of law, due process, and voting rights, famously said "Never, ever be afraid to make some noise and get in good trouble, necessary trouble."[34] An example of good trouble is when you're told to keep quiet but you lawfully protest against injustice. John McCain, a former POW, sometimes got into good trouble by supporting principled, bipartisan legislation as a U.S. senator.

Additionally, there are valuable lessons about hope, purpose, and significance that can be learned from the popular anime and manga series *Naruto*. The main character, Naruto Uzumaki, begins life as a lonely and outcast orphan in a ninja village. Despite being shunned, his goal is to become the Hokage, the respected leader of the village. Starting as a clumsy and mischievous underdog, Naruto grows through hard work, strong

---

[33] Wiersbe, *On Being a Leader for God.*
[34] Lewis, 2012 Commencement Address.

friendships, and the guidance of mentors. He learns advanced ninja techniques and overcomes major threats.

In one episode, Naruto reflects, "If no one acknowledged me and I stayed the way I was ... maybe I would have resented the village and everyone in it, and gone wild."[35] Eventually, he realized that every person is responsible for their own actions. Over time, he becomes a hero who unites both allies and former enemies, ultimately symbolizing purpose, competence, perseverance, and the pursuit of one's goals.

Oscar Wilde may not be accurate in adding the phrase "far more" to his famous statement "Life imitates art far more than art imitates life." Nevertheless, it is clear that life and art imitate each other to some extent, and that construction is better than destruction.

Setting and Achieving Goals

"To be successful and balanced, we should set goals in all areas of life."[36] As stated, knowing why you're here (Purpose) and where you are (Reality) can help you determine where you want to be (Destiny). Where you want to be in the future is an implied goal. But it needs more specificity to be a concrete possibility. "A goal is a dream with a deadline." It's a target to aim for.

"Begin with the end in mind,"[37] and work backward to structure your SMART goal: Specific, Measurable, Achievable, Relevant, and Time-bound. *What* is your dream goal, and *when* do you want to achieve it? *Where* do you want it to happen? Your purpose answers *why* you want to achieve that goal. A plan outlines *how* you'll get there. The process, integrated within the plan, breaks it down into actionable steps. A strategy is the method for executing the plan and process effectively.

---

[35] Date, "Uzumaki Naruto."

[36] Ngezahayo, *Essentials of Career Management for Language Professionals.*

[37] Covey, *7 Habits of Highly Effective People.*

When multiple processes work together, they form a system that supports consistency and efficiency. A productive SYSTEM is a mechanism that helps you **S**ave **Y**ourself **S**ome **T**ime, **E**nergy, and **M**oney. *Figure 2.2 illustrates this complete goal-setting approach.*

Figure 2.2 SMART Goal-Setting Framework

SMART Goal-Setting Framework		
Questions	**Components**	**Explanations**
What?	Goal	The desired achievement or destination
When?	Deadline	The timeframe or target date for completion
Where?	Location	The place and context for the results
Why?	Purpose	The reason you want to achieve the goal
How?	Plan	The customized road map
	Process	The steps within the map that guide you to the goal
	Strategy	The method for executing the plan and process
	System	The coordinated processes that move like gears

Using the GPS Map worksheet, you will create a total of four foundational goals: two personal and two professional. Later, you will connect the goals, especially those in the Purpose and Plan chapters.

Due to space constraints and the need to be concise, not all components of each goal will be explicitly addressed. For instance, in my upcoming *Goal I* example, I don't directly answer the questions *Why?* or *How?* However, the remaining components can be addressed through the other GPS questions or included in your optional side notes.

Instructions: Look in the Mirror Today

You'll create your Purpose Guiding Principle by answering a few questions. Try to keep your responses on a personal level, because later you'll create your professional purpose. Avoid using common, repetitive phrases, such as "I want to live life to the fullest." Don't beat yourself up if you're unsure about what your purpose is right now. It's fine if this is just your rough draft; you can refine it later. Try your best to only input one brief sentence for each question. The answer to the third question will serve as your first foundational goal.

Example

Why are you here on earth? (Utility)

I'm here to boost relationships with my faith, family, friends, and partner, while enhancing my planning and design thinking skills.

What stage of life are you in now? (Reality)

Currently, at 23, I feel stuck as I struggle to balance life as a parent, an employee, and a part-time student.

GOAL I

Where are you going and/or where do you want to be? (Vision and Destiny)

I envision becoming a healthier and more emotionally grounded homeowner, with at least two streams of income, within seven years.

Assemble

Fill in the blanks in the GPS Map with one brief sentence each.

Why are you here on earth? (Utility)

_____

_____

What stage of life are you in now? (Reality)

_____

_____

GOAL I:

Where are you going and/or where do you want to be? (Vision and Destiny)

_____

_____

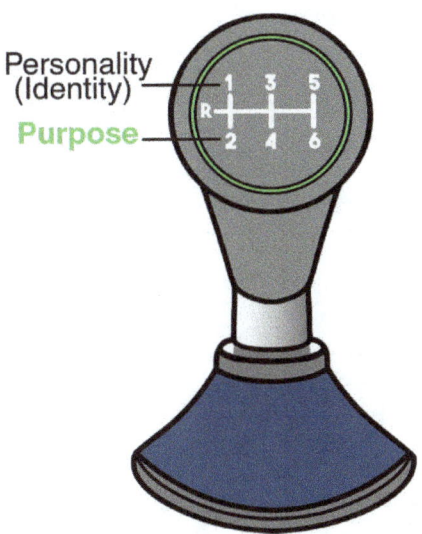

Practice: Reinforce Your Purpose GPS.

Shift: Symbolically shift into the Purpose GPS second gear.

Reinforce: For example, if you feel that there's little reason or meaning to life, you can memorize, repeat, and consistently live out your purpose in different ways. Based on the example provided, living out your purpose could look like taking quality time to plan and design engaging activities to enhance your relationships.

Describe and/or draw your own ways of how you can (and will) practice your Purpose GPS.

Discuss your thoughts with select people to reinforce what you've completed so far.

_____

_____

_____

_____

_____

_____

Chapter 3: Passion

"Passion to a person is what gas is to a car.
Without it, you won't go anywhere!"
–Alex Haditaghi

Description: What Drives You?

Beep Beep! Passion is like the turbo boost in a Formula 1 race car. It's that second wind that propels you forward when the road gets tough. Passion is the amount and the quality of the fuel that'll get you to your destination.

You should have a deep, burning passion for what you value, for those things you believe in and find meaningful. Your values should be like a spark plug igniting your desires that guide your decisions and actions.

It's also important to cultivate an "attitude of gratitude" and appreciation for your values. For example, a person who appreciates and values creativity might feel a strong passion for designing. Or a person who values leadership might feel a strong passion for mentoring others.

To understand what you truly value, observe how and where you *willingly* spend your time, energy, money, and resources. Pay attention to who and what occupies most of your thoughts and your daily life. Look at your receipts, social media usage and scrolling time, online search history, entertainment choices, commuting time, and places you frequent. These are all subtle yet telling indicators of what captures your attention and shapes your life. By evaluating how these activities align with your core values, you can get a clearer picture of where your heart truly is found. Then, decide if any of your activities or values need to be adjusted.

Once you've identified what you value, it becomes easier to align your daily actions with those values. This alignment will bring you a sense of fulfillment and purpose because you will be living in harmony with what matters most to you. Conversely, when your actions don't match your values, it can lead to feelings of dissatisfaction or even internal conflict.

It's important to remember that values aren't just abstract concepts. They should be reflected in your day-to-day choices, relationships, and goals. Living according to your values creates a more meaningful, intentional life.

Identifying Your Passion

Pause for a moment and think about your answer to this question: If you had to choose just one thing to do for the rest of your life, without getting paid for it, what would you do? The answer to that question might be your passion. Maybe it's time to rekindle a childhood passion or dream of yours. Don't worry, we'll discuss the importance of getting paid later.

Sir Ken Robinson was an educator, author, and advocate for creativity in education. In his book *Finding Your Element*, he writes, "The Element is the meeting point between natural aptitude and personal passion ... When people are in their Element, they connect with something fundamental to their sense of identity, purpose, and well-being."[38] Galloway adds to Robinson's statement when he says, "Your job is to find something you're good at, and after ten thousand hours of practice, get great at it. The emotional and economic rewards that accompany being great at something will make you passionate about whatever that something is."[39] The popular idea of "ten thousand hours" was notably popularized by Malcolm Gladwell in *Outliers*. Together, their insights suggest that both self-discovery and sustained effort are key to finding meaningful and fulfilling work.

Do not make the mistake of believing that passion automatically converts to profit. Many miss or do not consider the steps between the two to earn a living. Think about the starving artist. On the one hand, they have a passion for what they do, which is creating art, but on the other hand, the profit often doesn't match the great amount of time and effort they put into creating that art. Later on, you'll have the chance to connect your personal goals to your professional goals. That includes integrating your personal passion and values with your professional desires.

Job vs. Career vs. Calling

Some people have *jobs*. Others have *careers*. And still others are working at what they were called to do.

A *job* is what you do temporarily, as you bounce from one place of employment to another. When you ask someone if they like what they do, and they hesitate before responding like, "Well, it pays the bills ..." that generally means they have a *job*. A J-O-B is also known as Just Over Broke. Many employees with *jobs* work just enough so they don't get fired and get paid just enough so they won't quit.

---

[38] Robinson and Aronica, *Finding Your Element.*
[39] *The Algebra of Happiness.*

The next step up from a job is a *career*. A career is like running full speed in a hamster wheel. But keeping that pace will eventually cause boredom and burnout.

The next step up from a career is a *calling*. According to Greene,[40] "The word 'vocation' comes from the Latin and means 'to call or be called.' The original word, *vocare*, meant 'a calling from God to do spiritual work.'" Over the years, that meaning has expanded and some now view it as a calling into any occupation that a person feels drawn to. "For those who pursue a *calling,* their work is intrinsically rewarding in its own right—not just a means to an end. So, what you do professionally fulfills you personally as well."[41]

Happiness vs. Fulfillment

Having a passion can lead to a very fulfilling life. As the saying goes, happiness is temporary, but a life of passion and purpose creates lasting fulfillment.

Happiness is based on what is happening at the moment. Naturally, people feel happy when things are good and unhappy when things are not good. This is the transient nature of happiness: It's fleeting and it is often tied to external circumstances, which are constantly changing. Although it's great to experience happiness, it's important to recognize that it's not a permanent condition. That's because happiness depends on situations that can shift without warning. It's common for people to naturally say "I just want to be happy." That's fine, but sometimes unrealistic expectations can cause chronic disappointment when those expectations aren't met.

Fulfillment, on the other hand, is more stable and less dependent on these ever-changing situations. It is rooted in a sense of meaning and purpose that transcends temporary circumstances. When you live with passion, you are

---

[40] Robert Greene, *Mastery.*
[41] Kelley and Kelley, *Creative Confidence.*

deeply connected to something greater than the momentary highs and lows of life.

Fulfillment comes from knowing that your actions align with your values and that you are contributing to something that matters. Happiness should naturally flow from fulfillment.

Michael Jordan and Passion

From a young age, Michael Jordan exhibited a strong combination of natural talent and a determined will to succeed in sports. However, his journey to greatness didn't follow a straightforward path.

Michael Jordan's father, James Jordan, once reflected on his son's childhood by saying that Michael wasn't suited for a typical factory job; he would probably go hungry trying. As a kid, Michael would give away all his allowance to his siblings and even other neighborhood kids just to have them do his chores, often leaving himself with nothing. "Yet that laziness magically disintegrated when it came to sports. If it involved a ball in the air and a contest to be settled, the switch came on."[42] That's ignited passion!

This early glimpse into Michael's behavior highlights his deep passion for sports, but it also underscores his struggle to find direction. As a teenager, Michael imagined the possibility of becoming a professional athlete. It was one of the few things that truly captured his interest.

Despite the lack of a clear route to success, Michael's determination and natural talent ultimately allowed him to bridge the gaps between passion, hard work, and the professional world. Eventually, Jordan was able to integrate his natural talent for what he enjoyed doing with what he could get paid for, which ultimately made him one of the greatest athletes of all time.

---

[42] Lazenby, *Michael Jordan.*

Michael Jordan valued continuous improvement, his family relationships, and sports. Those values were demonstrated in his passion for basketball, his team, and winning. In the Netflix documentary *The Last Dance*, Jordan's former coach Phil Jackson and teammates like Scottie Pippen discuss how Jordan often took it upon himself to train intensively during off-seasons. Even though there were no games, he would still push his body and mind to the limit to stay in top form. His passion for being the best was reflected in his constant self-improvement and in challenging his teammates, even after winning multiple championships.

The Last Dance demonstrates that passion is a powerful force that can drive you to greatness, but it also shows that greatness requires discipline, determination, consistency, and sacrifice. It looks at how true passion isn't just about loving something; it requires a full commitment, even when the path is challenging.

Jordan achieved extraordinary success throughout his career. He led the Chicago Bulls to six NBA championships, and he personally won five MVP awards, cementing his legacy as a dominant force in the league. Known for his scoring prowess, Jordan led the league in points per game for ten seasons and was named Finals MVP every time he won a championship. He was also recognized for his defensive skills, earning NBA Defensive Player of the Year honors in 1988 and making the All-Defensive First Team nine times. Jordan represented the United States in the Olympics, winning two gold medals, and was inducted into the Basketball Hall of Fame in 2009.

Beyond basketball, Michael Jordan's cultural impact through his iconic Air Jordan sneakers and his global brand transcended sports, making him an enduring worldwide icon. Those are stacked clutch moves!

Jordan remains a source of great inspiration to many. On the other hand, his achievements might intimidate you. Remember that you might not be the most talented, the smartest, the best looking, or the one with the most resources, but you can still achieve greatness by being passionately consistent and working hard. "Grit has two components: passion and perseverance ... success [has] been all about passion and perseverance sustained over years and years."[43] Don't underestimate the underdog with that pit bull grit. "Hard work beats talent when talent fails to work hard" – Tim Notke.

Marc Anthony and Passion

Singer Marc Anthony's "Vivir Mi Vida" is a cheerful song about embracing passion and staying true to one's values. Through its upbeat rhythm, energetic melody, and inspiring lyrics, the song promotes a message of resilience, joy, and self-expression.

The phrase *vivir mi vida* translates to "live my life." The song's message revolves around letting go of negativity, overcoming challenges, and embracing life's opportunities. The lyrics encourage listeners to focus on enjoying life, dancing, and celebrating, regardless of the difficulties that may come their way.

The connection between your internal values and your external passion can lead to a powerful state known as "flow." This concept, introduced by psychologist Mihály Csíkszentmihályi, describes a mental state where you are fully immersed in an activity and experiencing deep enjoyment and focus. Many gamers and musicians have expressed this feeling.

Values provide the structure, and passion generates the flow. Both are needed for longevity. Sometimes there can be tension between those who prefer more order and others who prefer more spontaneity. That's why sometimes creative people will say, "Let's just go with the flow."

When you're in flow, time seems to disappear because you're so absorbed in what you're doing and the vibes are just right. It's like coasting downhill

---

[43] Duckworth, *Grit.*

effortlessly on a bike or skateboard on an easygoing day, where everything feels smooth and natural.

Flow isn't just about having the necessary skills. It's about loving what you're doing. When you're passionate about something, it doesn't feel like work; it feels like a fun, effortless ride. You have fun while getting it done.

Sometimes, adopting the right mindset can make it easier to tackle tasks you don't enjoy. "Mindset" means being fixed or set in the mind. It's a habitual way of thinking that can be productive or destructive. A set mind is like concrete that's been hardened for years. It can take some time with a jackhammer, so to speak, to break up negative stinkin' thinkin' in order to develop a new and constructive way of thinking.

People often find motivation, with the proper mindset, to do unpleasant chores like cleaning, laundry, grocery shopping, or homework when they pair them with music, singing, dancing, positive thinking, or conversation. To have fun while getting it done is a balanced approach to enjoying yourself while doing what you must. Having fun alone might not get the job done. And only getting it done might be boring. If you can't make it fun, at least try to stay engaged and focus on the benefits that the result of the task will bring.

Aligning Passion with Opportunities in Artificial Intelligence

In today's evolving job market, passion alone is not always enough; it often needs to be paired with the tools and technologies that are shaping the future of work. Microsoft's 2024 Work Trend Index, conducted in collaboration with LinkedIn, provides a comprehensive analysis of how artificial intelligence (AI) is reshaping the workplace. It gathered insights from a global survey of over 30,000 knowledge workers across 31 countries.

One of the survey results indicated that "66% of leaders say they wouldn't hire someone without AI skills."[44]

Regardless of what you think about AI, it's part of our lives. Although some may be reluctant, hiring managers, career counselors, educators, and learning and development trainers know the importance of training students and employees for AI-based employment opportunities.

The 2024 Adobe for Education Creative AI jobs report stated, "Creativity or creative problem-solving, as well as new communication across media, are the two important skills with the advent of AI, according to hiring managers and higher education educators. In part, these skills are seen as the most uniquely human, and so are viewed as augmentable, but not replaceable, by generative AI."[45]

It's important to consider niche creative problem-solving employment opportunities that align with your personality, purpose, and passion, where AI serves as a long-term supplement to your work, not a replacement for it.

---

[44] Microsoft and LinkedIn, *2024 Annual Work Trend Index.*
[45] Edelman and Adobe.

Instructions: Look to the Future Through the Windshield

You'll create your Passion Guiding Principle by answering some questions and using the Values Chart below, Figure 3.1. Choose your top 2-4 core values from the chart or from what you believe in and find worth in. You can also mix some words from the chart with your own words. They will be added to your answer for the first question. Try your best to only input one brief sentence for each question. The answer to the third question will serve as your second foundational goal.

Figure 3.1. Values Chart

Values Chart				
Accountability	Empathy	Growth	Justice	Perseverance
Authenticity	Excellence	Honesty	Leadership	Respect
Collaboration	Fairness	Humility	Learning	Responsibility
Community	Family	Humor	Love	Security
Confidence	Flexibility	Independence	Loyalty	Self-discipline
Courage	Forgiveness	Innovation	Mindfulness	Teamwork
Creativity	Generosity	Integrity	Optimism	Wisdom
Diversity	Gratitude	Joy	Patience	Work-life balance

Example

What do you value (believe in and find worth in)? (Appreciation)

I value gratitude, dependability, mutual respect, and the wise use of my time, energy, money, and resources.

What is your natural talent(s) and/or what do you really enjoy doing? (Motivation)

Creating art, designing, and executing plans for volunteer projects such as live community events are activities I enjoy.

GOAL II

Based on your previous answers, what's your preferred future profession? (Ambition)

I want to start as a company's project coordinator and transition into full-time and freelance project management (PM) roles.

Assemble

Fill in the blanks in the GPS Map with one brief sentence each.

What do you value (believe in and find worth in)? (Appreciation)

_____

_____

What is your natural talent(s) and/or what do you really enjoy doing? (Motivation)

_____

_____

GOAL II:

Based on your previous answers, what's your preferred future profession? (Ambition)

_____

_____

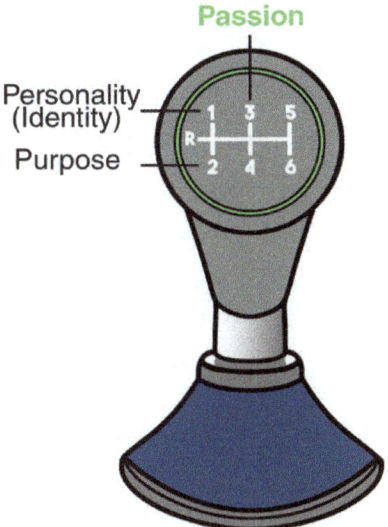

Practice: Reinforce Your Passion GPS

Shift: Symbolically shift into the Passion GPS third gear.

Reinforce: For example, unplug and take a digital detox. Take a walk in nature. Reflect on what has truly excited you, especially when you were younger. Play a board game with others.

Describe and/or draw your own ways of how you can and will practice your Passion GPS.

Discuss your thoughts with select people to reinforce what you've completed so far.

_____

_____

_____

_____

_____

_____

_____

_____

_____

_____

_____

_____

_____

_____

_____

_____

_____

_____

_____

_____

_____

_____

_____

_____

_____

_____

_____

_____

_____

_____

_____

_____

_____

_____

_____

_____

_____

Rest Stop 1: Personal Goals Summary

We'll exit the highway to relax and reflect during these rest stops. Then we'll lift the hood and check on how everything's running. Realize that you've already achieved a level of success if you completed and executed the exercises up to this point. In essence, you've unraveled and assembled your Personal GPS puzzle pieces. That also means that half of your treasure map is done. Now, let's take a look at the personal goals summary.

Identity is not about what you *do*; it's about who you *are*. It's not about titles, roles, appearances, or social media personas.

Identity is the foundation for purpose.

Purpose is why we're here on Earth. It is our reason for existing.

Values are foundational, like the roots of a tree, and are the place from which passion naturally grows.

So far, you've listed **who** you are, **where** you're from, **where** you are now, **why** you're here, and **where** you want to be. Now, you can create the steps for **how** to get there by leveling up to the Professional Goals of your GPS Map.

"Work life balance (WLB) is considered simply as a tradeoff between professional and personal life."[46]

---

[46] Sharma and Jha, "Work-Life Balance."

Professional Goals Introduction

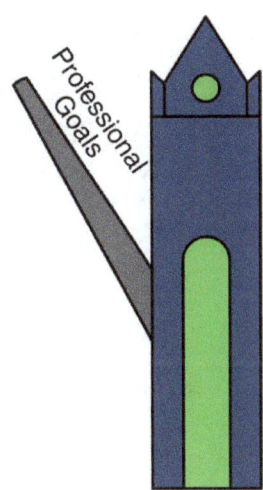

Your professional goals are on the other side of the work-life bridge. Your high-level Professional Goals for Problem-Solving, Planning, and Profit will be built upon your Personal Goals.

A good way to begin doing that is to conduct a brief SWOT analysis on yourself. SWOT stands for Strengths, Weaknesses, Opportunities, and Threats. Understanding your own internal strengths and areas for growth and recognizing external opportunities and threats can give you clearer direction and greater confidence when it comes to setting meaningful goals. This kind of self-awareness supports better decision-making and helps ensure that your professional ambitions are aligned with your personal foundation.

As you build this alignment, think of your professional (work) goals as being on one side of the scale and your personal (life) goals as being on the other side of the scale. Success means balancing the time and tasks for each side in the best possible way.

Some companies promote a work-life balance culture, which is commendable. Yet, others operate under the belief that "Work-life balance is not an entitlement or benefit. Your company cannot give it to you. You have to create it for yourself."[47]

Achieving balance is not a one-time event. It is an ongoing process of adjusting priorities. When both your personal well-being and your professional progress are valued and supported, long-term sustainability and satisfaction are much more likely to follow.

---

[47] Kelly, *Off Balance.*

Chapter 4: Problem-Solving

"The best way to escape from a problem is to solve it."
–Brendan Francis

Description: Is Your Check Engine Light On?

Pump your brakes! The smell of smoke and scorched tires floats in the air. People can overheat and malfunction just like cars, especially on laborious journeys. You don't ignore your car's "check engine" light, do you? That light indicates there's a real problem with your vehicle.

It's really no different from a person having the first signs of sickness, such as constant coughing, sneezing, fever, and high blood pressure. First there's the indicator light, which can be any of the symptoms just mentioned; then the diagnosis; then the prescription; and finally, the application to solve the problem. Problems and pain are part of life, but there's pleasure in the solutions. Take calculated risks and turn failures, rejections, and roadblocks into new, alternative routes.

For you, while on the road to success, problem-solving is like a pit stop. It's about finding solutions that keep you moving forward, even when you hit a bump in the road or get a flat tire. Every good road trip can have unexpected detours. Sometimes a mechanic or tow truck might be needed to assist. The best professionals don't drive on fumes; they tackle challenges head-on and find ways to solve problems, innovate, and improve.

Also, it's important to consider how you can help others in your profession, whatever that may be. A practical way to do this is by helping other people (or other companies) solve problems. Companies value creative problem-solvers, as solving problems benefits everyone. Adopting this mindset can benefit you as well as Human Resources managers and Learning and Development trainers, especially when it comes to recruiting, onboarding, engaging, and retaining employees.

Helping others leads to mutual satisfaction. This mutual benefit not only strengthens relationships but builds trust and credibility in your field. When your skills contribute to someone else's success, your value increases not just as a professional, but as a person who makes a positive impact.

Over time, this approach can lead to new opportunities and partnerships as well as a deeper sense of fulfillment in your work. Helping others isn't just good ethics. It's good strategy for long-term success and purpose-driven growth.

Dr. Ignaz Semmelweis on Solving the Germ Problem

Keep in mind that you might want to solve problems that others don't see or pretend not to see. Naturally, we must first acknowledge that a problem exists before we can attempt to fix it. "Facts do not cease to exist because they are ignored." –Aldous Huxley.

An example is Ignaz Semmelweis, a nineteenth-century Hungarian physician who discovered that handwashing with disinfectant drastically reduced maternal deaths from childbed fever. While working in a Vienna hospital, he observed that doctors were spreading deadly infections from autopsies to childbirth patients. When he mandated handwashing, mortality rates dropped sharply. However, his findings were mocked as unscientific and rejected by the medical establishment, which was unwilling to accept the truth. Isolated and eventually committed to an asylum, he died in obscurity. Years after his death, Louis Pasteur's germ theory and Joseph Lister's antiseptic methods proved Semmelweis was right.

Lesser-Known Problem Solvers

Over the years, many problem solvers including engineers, inventors, scientists, and everyday people have made significant contributions to society without receiving the recognition they deserved. Dr. Gladys West used satellite data modeling in the 1980s to accurately map the Earth's surface, laying the foundation for modern GPS. Dr. Thomas Mensah revolutionized fiber optic cable production in the early 1980s by speeding up manufacturing and easing a major telecommunications bottleneck. Ada Lovelace is credited with probably creating the world's first computer algorithm in the 1800s, enabling machines to perform general tasks beyond calculation. Born in 1893, Gopalswamy Doraiswamy Naidu, with only an elementary education, developed a high-efficiency electric motor, created low-cost farming tools, and founded an institute to teach practical engineering.

Frederick McKinley Jones invented refrigerated trucks in 1940, preserving perishables during transit and transforming the cold chain system. Alfredo Zolezzi Garretón developed the Plasma Water Sanitation System in 2011 to provide safe drinking water in underserved communities, reflecting his "Innovation with Purpose" philosophy. Gerald "Jerry" Lawson created the first commercial video game console with interchangeable cartridges in 1976, solving the problem of games being hardwired into systems and changing the future of home gaming.

Marvin Gaye Wanted to Know "What's Going On"

What's Going On is an iconic album that Marvin Gaye released in 1971. Before that release, Gaye had been primarily known for his smooth, romantic soul music. But deeply affected by the turmoil in the world around him, Gaye became increasingly frustrated by the social and political issues of the time and sought to use his music as a vehicle for social change.

Initially, Berry Gordy, the founder of Motown Records, strongly opposed the production of Marvin Gaye's song "What's Going On." Gordy was reluctant to release the song because it was a significant departure from the usual Motown style, which was primarily focused on love songs and commercial hits. Gordy feared that Gaye's new song would alienate the Motown audience and damage the brand's reputation.

Gaye initially recorded "What's Going On" without Berry Gordy's approval. Gaye persisted and the song was eventually released in 1971. Gordy's initial opposition proved to be baseless, and the song went on to become a major hit. The album of the same name became one of the most successful albums in music history. The song's success helped redefine both Gaye's career and Motown's legacy.

Some of the lyrics were:

> You see, war is not the answer
> For only love can conquer hate

Tears for Fears Sing "Everybody Wants to Rule the World"

The Tears for Fears song "Everybody Wants to Rule the World" inspires listeners to think critically about the potential problem of unchecked power. Despite its upbeat musical arrangement, the song carries a bittersweet tone. The music's blend of optimism and melancholy mirrors the message of the lyrics: power and control can seem like an ideal, but they come with heavy emotional, moral, and social costs. It hints that it's better to focus on shared goals and cooperation rather than on foolish pride, selfishness, greed, and jealousy.

Upon its release, the song became a massive international hit. It reached number one on the Billboard Hot 100 in the United States and charted high in many other countries. It became a defining anthem of the 1980s, gaining widespread radio play and cementing its place in pop music history.

George Orwell and The Animal Farm

Not only do people want to rule the world, but animals do too! *Animal Farm* is a book written by George Orwell and published in 1945. It is a political allegory about animals who overthrow their human farmer to create a society based on equality, but the pigs gradually take control, becoming as oppressive as the humans they replaced. As the pigs grow more powerful, they manipulate the truth, rewrite the rules, and exploit the other animals, leading to the chilling realization: "All animals are equal, but some animals are more equal than others."[48] This phrase is a paradox, a statement that contradicts itself, and is meant to expose hypocrisy and the abuse of power.

As Acton famously said, "Absolute power corrupts absolutely."[49] The story mirrors real-world events, such as revolutions where calls for justice turn into new forms of oppression, showing how power can corrupt and how ideals of equality can be twisted for control. This story serves as a timeless warning

---

[48] Orwell, *Animal Farm.*
[49] Dalberg, *Historical Essays and Studies.*

about the fragility of freedom and the ease with which it can be undermined. "Those who cannot remember the past are condemned to repeat it."[50]

The Message in *Hamilton: An American Musical*

In the musical *Hamilton*, the song "History Has Its Eyes on You" features a pivotal moment where George Washington imparts a crucial lesson to Alexander Hamilton. Washington reflects on his own early military failures and emphasizes the weight of legacy and the unpredictable nature of history. He warns Hamilton that his actions will be scrutinized by history, encapsulating this with the phrase "history has its eyes on you."[51] This advice becomes a central pattern in the show, underscoring the theme that individuals must act with caution, knowing that their choices will be scrutinized by future generations. It also highlights the value of unbiased and nonpartisan investigative journalism because it records historical moments that profoundly affect the public.

Value Proposition Design

The book *Value Proposition Design* by Alexander Osterwalder and his coauthors provides a detailed, customer-centric approach to problem-solving. By using structured tools like the Value Proposition Canvas, the book helps the reader to identify core customer problems, generate creative solutions, validate those solutions with real customers, and effectively communicate value. This approach ensures that problem-solving is targeted, innovative, and aligned with both customer needs and business goals.

This is relevant because it shifts the focus from simply offering a product or service to truly understanding what customers value and need. Rather than assuming what might work, it encourages empathy, research, and iteration: key traits in effective problem-solving. When businesses apply

---

[50] Santayana, *The Life of Reason*, 284.
[51] Miranda, *Hamilton*.

this mindset, they're more likely to create solutions that resonate deeply with their target audience and build lasting loyalty. Ultimately, *Value Proposition Design* empowers professionals to create meaningful, relevant offerings that deliver real impact and drive sustainable success.

Creative Problem-Solving with Artificial Intelligence

"Creative confidence is a way of experiencing the world that generates new approaches and solutions."[52] Creative confidence can be developed and applied to creative problem-solving in order to find innovative solutions. As the saying goes, *if it isn't broken, don't fix it.* But if it can be improved, modify it. And if it doesn't exist, build it. That requires divergent thinking rather than a dichotomous mindset.

A dichotomous mindset is limiting because it frames solutions as either one thing or another, instead of recognizing the possibility of creative combinations that incorporate both. This limited perspective is being challenged in the workforce, where adaptability and a broader skill set are becoming essential.

"Workers and employers not only recognize the need for generative AI training, but also the importance of creative problem-solving skills that complement generative AI and digital skills and cannot currently be easily replicated by technology."[53]

The HBR guide to generative AI for managers contains insightful approaches to using generative AI as a copilot or co-thinker for problem-solving and root cause analysis. "You can ask *gen AI* to help you and your team understand various methods of root cause analysis such as the 'five whys' technique, fishbone diagrams [Ishikawa diagram], fault tree analysis and others."[54] This makes it much easier to systematically identify the true

---

[52] Kelley and Kelley, *Creative Confidence.*
[53] Edelman and Adobe, *2024 Creative AI Jobs Report.*
[54] Farri and Rosani, *HBR Guide to Generative AI for Managers.*

causes of issues rather than merely reacting to symptoms, enabling teams to design deeper, more durable solutions.

Figure 4.1 illustrates practical problem-solving tools and techniques that can be used alongside generative AI to clarify problems and generate multiple potential solutions. For example, a retail company facing long wait times and low satisfaction scores combines high-quality AI prompts with design thinking to address this common customer service challenge:

- **Empathize:** Analyze customer feedback with AI to identify key pain points.

- **Define:** Clarify the issue as inefficient handling of routine inquiries.

- **Ideate:** Generate ideas and decide to implement an AI-powered chatbot to automate basic queries.

- **Prototype:** Develop and test the AI chatbot to improve response quality.

- **Test:** Use AI analytics to refine the system based on real user interactions.

Figure 4.1. Problem-Solving Tools and Techniques

Problem-Solving Tools and Techniques	
Mind Map –	Brainstorm multiple causes and solutions around a central problem.
Flow Chart –	Map linear process steps to pinpoint errors, delays, or inefficiencies.
The 5 Whys –	Ask "why" at least five times to trace the root cause of the problem.
Ishikawa Diagram –	Identify the problem, classify causes (e.g. people, processes, machines), and analyze to find the root issues.
Design Thinking –	Focus on user needs through empathy, defining the problem, ideation, prototyping, and testing.

Solving Math Problems in Hidden Figures

Hidden Figures (2016) is a film that showcases the true stories of three women, Katherine Johnson, Dorothy Vaughan, and Mary Jackson, who played key roles in the success of NASA's space missions during the early years of the US space program. Throughout the film, the central characters face significant obstacles ranging from racial and gender discrimination to societal expectations that limit their potential.

For example: Katherine Johnson's work was crucial to calculating trajectories for John Glenn's orbital flight. However, because she was a woman in the 1960s, she had to overcome institutional barriers, such as being excluded from meetings or having to work in segregated spaces.

Yet the women found ways to overcome this. Katherine Johnson worked closely with her team, particularly with her supportive colleague, Al Harrison, to calculate complex flight paths. Dorothy Vaughan took the initiative to teach herself and others about programming computers, which was a critical skill for the success of NASA's missions.[55]

And things did change as a result of this movie. The film motivated the Walt Disney Company to partner with the US State Department on the "Hidden No More" exchange program. The film also inspired initiatives beyond the United States. In 2019, the third annual "Hidden No More" exchange program brought fifty women from around the world who have excelled in STEM careers to the United States to discuss strategies to promote the achievements of women in those fields.[56]

Developing Problem-Solving Skills with Minecraft

The video game *Minecraft* can work well as a tool to develop problem-solving skills due to its open-ended gameplay, the variety of challenges it offers, and the necessity for creativity, planning, and adaptability. Whether

---

[55] Melfi, *Hidden Figures.*
[56] Walt Disney Company, "Partners with U.S. State Department."

through building, survival, or exploration, players are constantly engaging with problems that require innovative thinking, resource management, collaboration, and resilience. By engaging with *Minecraft*, players can develop key problem-solving competencies that extend well beyond the game. They learn skills that can be applied to real-world challenges.

Additionally, *Minecraft*'s "sandbox" environment encourages experimentation without the fear of failure, allowing players to learn through trial and error. This freedom nurtures a growth mindset where mistakes are seen as opportunities to improve rather than as setbacks.

Joel Levin, a former school teacher and lifelong video game enthusiast, cofounded *MinecraftEdu* by merging his passion for gaming with a strong commitment to improving education. Levin's purpose was to address a major problem in education: student disengagement. He envisioned an educational environment where students could explore concepts collaboratively, creatively, and interactively. The result was *MinecraftEdu*, a modified version of *Minecraft* tailored for classroom use. The platform includes lesson plans, teacher tools, and support for integrating the game into various subject areas. It has empowered educators to harness the immersive nature of Minecraft to teach topics ranging from math and science to history.[57]

Levin and his team not only addressed a problem but also created a successful business. *MinecraftEdu* licenses were sold to schools worldwide, generating revenue while making a meaningful impact on how students learn. In 2016, Microsoft acquired *MinecraftEdu* and used it to launch *Minecraft: Education Edition*, expanding its reach to millions of students around the globe. This case illustrates how **passion** and **purpose** can come together to tackle real-world **problems** and build a sustainable, **profitable**

---

[57] Alawajee and Delafield-Butt, "Minecraft in Education."

venture in the education technology sector. Those are multiple clutch moves.

Professional Purpose

It's important to know how to solve problems based on your own Personality, Purpose, and Passion. In addition, it's critical to know *why* you want to solve these problems. Sinek states, "The best organizations and leaders start with why."[58] However, the approach in this book diverges slightly, as the "why" (professional purpose) is centered on *you*, not necessarily an organization.

When you discover *why* a problem matters to you personally, it becomes more than just an issue to fix; it becomes a mission worth pursuing. It's not just about solving a problem for the sake of solving it, but about understanding the deeper reason that motivates you to solve it. When you're clear on your "why," your actions gain clarity and consistency. Then others are more likely to connect with your vision and support your efforts.

Sharing your "why" is equally important because it invites others into your mission. When people understand the heart behind what you're doing, when they understand why it matters to *you* and why it should matter to *them*, it builds trust and engagement. A clearly communicated purpose attracts like-minded people who want to be part of something meaningful. Whether you're leading a team, starting a project, or launching a business, your "why" becomes a connection to the world around you.

Pause and ponder the following questions. From your experience, is there a type of problem that you are objectively good at solving? Do you think it's part of your vocation (calling) to solve these sorts of problems?

---

[58] Sinek, *Start with Why*, 57.

Instructions: Run the Diagnostic Test

You'll create your Problem-Solving Guiding Principle by answering some questions. State **only** the problem for now; later on, we'll discuss a potential solution. If not otherwise stated, don't feel the need to use citations or the same words from the examples to create your own principles.

Example

What customer-based problem can you solve, or what need can you fulfill, with your Personality, Purpose, and Passion while pursuing your profession? (Creativity)

Research suggests there's a shortage of effective creative project managers who can consistently deliver quality products to satisfied stakeholders, within scope, time, and budget.[59]

Why do you want to solve the problem or fulfill the need? (Professional Purpose: Why?)

I believe in continuous improvement and giving customers the best value for the price they pay.

What is the value proposition (the benefit for your customers) if you fix their problem? (Mutual Satisfaction)

The value proposition (benefit) is to efficiently deliver a balance of human-centric, data-driven results that will foster happy customers.

---

[59] Pinhas, "Project Management Statistics."

Assemble

Fill in the blanks in the GPS Map with one brief sentence each.

What customer-based problem can you solve, or what need can you fulfill, with your Personality, Purpose, and Passion while pursuing your profession? (Creativity)

_____

_____

Why do you want to solve the problem or fulfill the need? (Professional Purpose: Why?)

_____

_____

What is the value proposition (the benefit for your customers) if you fix their problem? (Mutual Satisfaction)

_____

_____

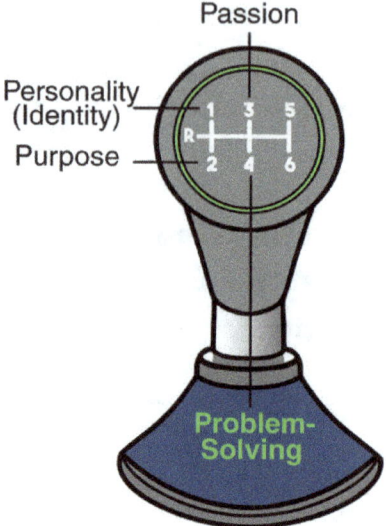

Practice: Reinforce Your Problem-Solving GPS

Shift: Symbolically shift into the Problem-Solving GPS fourth gear.

Reinforce: You can do this when you solve puzzles, read mysteries, play challenging games, etc. Brainstorm how to solve a specific problem with one of the problem-solving tools and techniques.

Describe and/or draw your own ways of how you can (and will) practice your Problem-Solving GPS now.

Discuss your ideas with select people to reinforce what you've completed so far.

_____

_____

_____

_____

_____

_____

_____

_____

Chapter 5: Plan

"A goal without a plan is just a wish"
–Attributed to Antoine de Saint-Exupéry

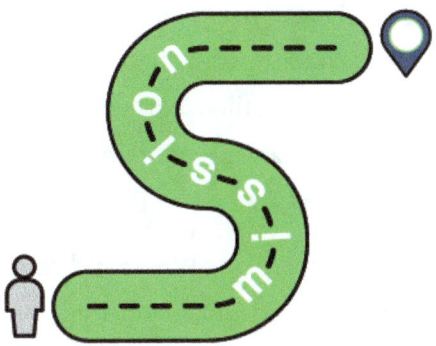

Description: Are We There Yet?

It's critical to have a plan before a long road trip. You must know your destination, you must have reliable directions, and you must know the locations where you can get gas, food, and a place to rest. Otherwise, how can you track and measure your progress toward your goal?

You can do this advance planning with a map and later compare what you planned to your real-time GPS navigation status. The worldwide cargo delivery services such as FedEx and UPS all have logistical plans for delivering packages around the globe so they can get the cargo where it's supposed to go.

You also need a plan if you're going to arrive at the place in life where you want to be. "Success is where preparation and opportunity meet" (attributed to racecar driver Bobby Unser). Have opportunities passed you by because you were unprepared? Think about it. It seems that many people focus solely on living in the moment with little to no planning for the future, while others are consumed by future planning and never stop to enjoy the memorable moments. How about balancing both according to the situation and requirements?

"Planning is of the essence when it comes to balancing your professional and personal life."[60] A haphazard life yields haphazard results. Convincing yourself that winging it all the time is the best approach isn't sustainable. It often leads to unnecessary, self-inflicted stress. Unless you are content to spend your life hoping things magically work out for you, you have to map out a way to get you from point A to point B in a manner that benefits you.

Crawl, walk, then run with the plan. Where did Amazon's business start and what did they sell? They did not begin by running a large business selling countless different products. No, they started in a garage selling physical books.

Think big. Start small. Do now. Sometimes people try to think big and start big. Then they get overwhelmed and quit. Psychologically, small successes breed bigger successes. It can boost your confidence and ability to do bigger and better. Don't aim for perfection. Aim for progress through iteration. Recalibrate and reroute when things don't go according to your plan. Sometimes you march, and other times you pivot in real-time to free-style. Those are clutch moves for GPS drivers.

---

[60] Ngezahayo, *Essentials of Career Management.*

SKAN Development

Your plan should include development through Skills, Knowledge, Attitude, and Networking (SKAN). That can be done through education, training, and practice. All of us have different SKAN levels. For example, someone might have high levels of skill, knowledge, and networking abilities but have a rotten attitude, especially when receiving feedback. That can hinder major opportunities. The good thing is that attitudes can be improved. Incorporating SKAN development into your plan ensures that you are not only prepared to tackle current challenges but also equipped to adapt to future opportunities. By intentionally identifying which skills and competencies are most relevant to your goals, you can focus your efforts where they will have the greatest impact.

In reference to networking, it's not only what you know, but who you know. Furthermore, it's about who knows you.

Regular self-assessment and reflection can help track your growth and reveal areas that need improvement. Over time, a strong SKAN foundation enhances both your personal confidence and your professional credibility, making you more effective in problem-solving and more competitive in your field. Continuously developing life skills can upskill your potential.

In addition, an assessment such as the Truity Career Aptitude Test could be helpful for your SKAN development.

John Maxwell on Planning and Leadership

Your plan should have a solution for your identified problem and align with your desired profession. That's your mission, which is *what* you're doing now or what you're going to do later. The strategy is *how* you're going to do it.

Being the driver of the car means that you are in charge of where the car goes. You are the leader. You are the one who has to create the plan for your GPS journey.

Throughout John Maxwell's speaking engagements and books, such as *Developing the Leader Within You 2.0*, he emphasizes that it is crucial to have a plan in life and in leadership. Maxwell discusses the importance of creating a roadmap for personal and professional growth and discusses how a plan serves as a guide for leaders and for those they influence.

Maxwell states that effective leaders must have a clear vision for where they want to go. Having a plan is a practical way of turning that vision into actionable steps. Without a written plan, even the most inspiring vision will remain nothing more than an abstract idea. It won't become something that can be acted upon and brought into reality.

A well-thought-out plan allows leaders to prioritize effectively. It keeps them working on the right tasks at the right times, which reduces wasted effort and helps achieve results more efficiently. It ensures that leaders are not working *re*actively but *pro*actively, with a clear roadmap that supports their vision and goals.

In addition, having a solid plan can help to defeat something called "imposter syndrome," a psychological pattern where individuals doubt their accomplishments and fear being exposed as frauds, even after they have attained what appears to be real success with plenty of external validation. People with imposter syndrome often believe they've only succeeded due to luck, timing, or other external factors rather than because of their own talent or effort. They often fear trying to repeat their success, thinking that this time they will surely fail and be "found out."

To some extent, that exemplifies a level of humility, and being humble is important. However, humility needs to be balanced with the confidence that you can do it, or you have done it before, and you can do it again. "Plan it, schedule it, and do follow-through consistently."[61]

---

[61] Maxwell, *Developing the Leader Within You.*

Clint Eastwood on Finishing Projects Within Scope, Time, and Budget

Clint Eastwood is one of the few people who has been successful in the film industry as an actor, producer, and director. "He's become known for filming with remarkable speed and economy. Of the 26 films Malpaso [Eastwood's production company] had made since 1968, not one had finished behind schedule or over budget."[62] That's a demonstration of using hard skills efficiently. But he is also known for exercising his soft skills (leadership skills) effectively. During an interview, Eastwood said, "I try to stimulate everyone to be as creative as they possibly can. I like them to contribute to the film and not just do their jobs by rote."[63]

In the 2008 movie *Gran Torino*, Walt Kowalski (Clint Eastwood) is living in a declining Detroit neighborhood. Divorced, isolated, and bitter, he harbors resentment toward his changing community, especially the Hmong immigrant families who have moved in next door. The Hmong were from Vietnam. They assisted the American soldiers during the Vietnam War.

Walt's life takes a turn when Thao, a shy Hmong teenager, is pressured by a local gang to steal from Walt as part of a gang initiation. Walt catches him in the act but doesn't press charges. Instead, he begins to form an unlikely bond with Thao and his family.

As Walt witnesses the dangers Thao faces from the gang, he becomes a reluctant mentor, teaching him about work and responsibility. Over time, Walt softens and begins to confront his own prejudices and regrets. The film builds to a powerful ending. It addresses themes such as redemption and cultural understanding.

---

[62] Gentry, "When Shooting Starts."
[63] Gentry.

Movie critic Kenneth Turan said, "The notion of a 78-year-old action hero may sound like a contradiction in terms, but Eastwood brings it off, even if his toughness is as much verbal as physical."[64]

Figure 5.1 illustrates Eastwood's workflow and successful execution of his plan as an actor, co-producer, and director.

Figure 5.1. Clint Eastwood's Plan and Results for Gran Torino

Clint Eastwood's Plan and Results for Gran Torino Movie	
Budget	$33 million (Low for Warner Brothers Pictures)
Box Office	$270 million (Commercial success)
Shoot Duration	35 days (Finished ahead of schedule)
Reshoots	Minimal
Scope Management	Limited locations and limited complex scenes
Production Style	Prepared, quiet set, few takes, impactful storytelling
Lean Methodology	Used local, first-time actors and Hmong community
Co-producers	Clint Eastwood, Malpaso Productions, etc.
Director and Actor	Clint Eastwood
Writer	Nick Schenk

7 Days Out Planning Example

The Netflix series *7 Days Out* takes viewers behind the scenes of significant live events, focusing on the preparation and planning that go into making them successful. Each episode highlights a different event and emphasizes how meticulous planning was the key to achieving success.

Episode 2 shows the grand reopening of the Eleven Madison Park Restaurant in New York City. The restaurant's team planned a complete overhaul. This required not only redesigning the menu but rethinking the entire dining experience, from sourcing the ingredients to working out the logistics of preparing and serving the food. The interior was redesigned

---

[64] Turan, "Review: Gran Torino."

with a minimalist, modern aesthetic, updating furniture, lighting, and decor while maintaining the restaurant's iconic essence to offer a fresh experience for diners. The kitchen was also reconfigured to improve workflow which played a key role in ensuring the Michelin-level quality of the restaurant's culinary offerings.

The planning involved coordination across many departments, from kitchen staff to front-of-house personnel, to ensure that the experience aligned with their new vision. The team employed a detailed punch list to track tasks and responsibilities, which facilitated effective coordination between team members. Natasha McIrvin, the restaurant's director of creative projects, played a pivotal role in managing this process.

This episode demonstrates how a restaurant's reopening and entire brand revamp involves careful planning of every detail, from food prep to customer service, and how this was absolutely necessary for the success of this operation, especially given the intense time constraints.[65]

Planning with Generative Artificial Intelligence

There are numerous planning and project management tools and techniques. All have benefits and drawbacks. One good option for its simplicity and broad use among multiple industries is Trello, a visual planning tool that becomes even more effective when combined with generative AI. Its intuitive board and card system helps organize tasks, track progress, and aid collaboration with others. When paired with AI tools, users can quickly generate task lists, content, and project outlines, then structure them in Trello for clear execution. AI can also assist in drafting reports, automating updates, and summarizing meetings, making planning faster and more efficient.

Using Trello with a Kanban board for a marketing campaign provides a clear, visual way to manage tasks. A Kanban board is a project management

---

[65] Warren, *7 Days Out.*

tool that organizes work into columns representing different stages of progress, typically labeled Backlog, To Do, In Progress, Review, and Completed. Tasks such as "Design social media ads" are created as cards, assigned to team members, given due dates, and tracked as they move through each stage. Features like labels, checklists, and automation help streamline the workflow and keep the team aligned.

AI tools including Butler AI, Trello's built-in automation assistant, enhance this process. On the Trello Kanban board, AI can automatically prioritize tasks by analyzing deadlines and dependencies. For example, it may move high-priority tasks like "Create blog post" to the top of the "To Do" list based on urgency. Butler AI can automate routine actions such as moving cards when checklists are completed, sending reminders, or creating recurring tasks. Additionally, predictive analytics can forecast realistic timelines and adjust due dates when tasks are delayed or resources are stretched. This intelligent automation ensures that key deliverables like "Design social media ads" stay on track and bottlenecks are minimized.

Personal Brand

Part of your plan includes developing your personal brand. A personal brand is different from a professional brand for a business. "Personal branding refers to those aspects of your personality that distinguish you from other professionals in the marketplace."[66] Essentially, it's how you differentiate yourself from others, showcasing what makes you memorable in your professional and personal life. It's critical to construct your own, which you will do soon.

---

[66] Indeed Editorial Team, "What Is Personal Branding?"

Using Video Games to Develop Planning Skills

Mobile games like *Pocket City 2* and *RollerCoaster Tycoon* are great for developing planning and problem-solving skills because they combine creative thinking with strategic decision-making.

In *RollerCoaster Tycoon*, you have to manage both money and resources. Keeping track of how much you're spending on rides, decorations, and staff while still ensuring the park remains profitable helps with budgeting and prioritization skills.

The game requires you to think ahead about park development, not just in the short term (building a single ride) but also in terms of park layout, guest satisfaction, and growth. To ensure long-term success, you have to consider factors like crowd flow, ride placement, and keeping guests happy.

The game's time-sensitive nature can teach you how to prioritize tasks effectively. You often have to decide whether to take a financial risk (like building an expensive roller coaster) or play it safe and simply go with the rides you already have. Evaluating the potential rewards and consequences improves decision-making and resource management abilities.

The Eclectic Product Development (EPD) Life Cycle and the Fusion PM Methodology

Part of your plan could include producing a product or service, such as an App, to help solve the problem. Replicable frameworks and methodologies can assist you with the production process. For example: "Lester Frederick created the Eclectic Product Development (EPD) Life Cycle [Figure 5.2]. The EPD Life Cycle is a hybrid life cycle that can foster efficiency, consistency, and creativity for managing M.E.T.A. [Media, Entertainment, Technology, and Art] projects."[67] The EPD Life Cycle is displayed below in the first column alongside other life cycles.

---

[67] Verzuh, *The Fast Forward MBA.*

Figure 5.2. Media, Entertainment, Tech, and Art (M.E.T.A.) Lifecycles

Media, Entertainment, Tech & Art (M.E.T.A.) Life Cycles			
Eclectic Product Development Life Cycle	**Video/Film Production Life Cycle**	**Game Development Life Cycle**	**Music Production Life Cycle**
Define	**Development**	**Initiation**	**Conceive**
Product Definition / Concept	Green-lighted Script	High Concept Doc	*Conception (e.g. Lyrics, Theme)*
Design	**Pre-production**	**Pre-production**	**Compose & Arrange**
(UX) Design Doc / Lo-Fi Sample	Script Breakdown Sheet	GDD & Lo-Fi Prototype	Rhythm, Melody, Harmony
Develop	**Production**	**Production**	**Edit**
Minimum Viable Product	Raw Video Footage	Alpha	Demo / Enhanced Song(s)
Detect (Test)	**Post Production**	**Iterative Testing**	**Mix**
Iterative Hi-Fi Prototype	Edited Video Footage	Beta	Stereo Song(s)
Deliver	**Distribution**	**Release**	**Master & Release**
Final Product or Service	Final Motion Picture	Gold Master Version	Cohesive Hi-Fi Song/EP/LP
Debrief & Determine	**Debrief**	**Post Mortem**	**Debrief**
Lessons Learned Register	*On-going Dailies*	*Review Notes*	*On-going Discussions*
Title for the role of project manager			
(Digital) PM, Producer, Team Lead, or Agile Coach	(Unit) Production Manager or Line Producer	Game Producer	A&R Manager or Music Producer
Key Deliverable(s) or Milestones			

© Lester Frederick, 2020

The Fusion Project Management (PM) Methodology was also created by Frederick: "The Fusion PM Methodology's phase titles and the EPD Life Cycle's phase titles are the same to promote consistency and clarity."[68]

There are more details about the EPD Life Cycle and the Fusion PM Methodology in Chapter 14 of *The Fast Forward MBA in Project Management* (6th ed.), which Frederick and Verzuh cowrote.

A book by Keith and Shonkwiler titled *Creative Agility Tools: 100+ Tools for Creative Innovation and Teamwork* works well with the EPD Life Cycle

---

[68] Verzuh.

and the Fusion PM Methodology because many of the tools are used to increase efficiency throughout the project's and the product's development life cycles.

Incorporating such frameworks into your planning allows you to organize your project into manageable phases, with built-in milestones for evaluation and continuous improvement. This approach also reduces the likelihood of wasted resources by ensuring that your work remains aligned with your goals and the needs of your target audience. In addition, abstract ideas can turn into structured action steps that can lead to tangible, high-quality results.

Instructions: Follow The Path

Your plan also needs steps to advance your vision and destiny. Stop and reverse back to your Personal Goals. Review them, especially those in the Purpose and Passion chapters, to refresh your memory. Then return to this section to continue. That's how your Plan can integrate your personal and professional goals, guiding you from where you are to where you want to be. In addition, all of your answers up to this point will help in creating your personal brand. The answer to the first question will serve as your third foundational goal.

Example

GOAL III

What's your executable Plan to solve the Problem using your Personality, Purpose, and Passion? (Mission)

My values-based solution and mission are to acquire PM tools, techniques, and templates to optimize my teamwork and PM skills, preparing me for future career opportunities.

Briefly, how, when, and where can you solve the Problem while pursuing your profession? (Strategy)

My strategy is to participate in school and online internships over the next 1-2 years to develop skills in scheduling, budgeting, tracking, and leadership.

Personal Brand Template and Example

Template: I want to be, or I am, a(n) <u>title</u> who assists <u>type of people or organizations</u> by <u>valuable service provided</u>.

Personal Brand: I want to be a <u>Digital Project Manager</u> who assists <u>multimedia clients</u> by <u>fulfilling their measurable success criteria</u>.

Assemble

Fill in the blanks with one brief sentence each.

GOAL III:

What's your executable Plan to solve the Problem with your Personality, Purpose, and Passion? (Mission)

_____

_____

Briefly, how, when, and where can you solve the Problem while pursuing your profession? (Strategy)

_____

_____

Personal Brand:

I want to be a _____

who assists _____

by _____.

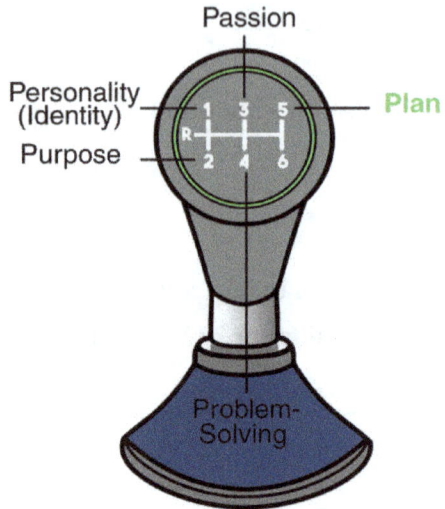

Practice: Reinforce Your Plan GPS

Shift: Symbolically shift into the Plan GPS fifth gear.

Reinforce: Practice by playing a board game like Ticket to Ride. Create a simple plan with a pen and paper or a project management tool like Trello. Execute the plan. Track and compare the plan to the actual results.

Describe and/or draw your own ways of how you can (and will) practice your Plan GPS.

Discuss your thoughts with select people to reinforce what you've completed so far.

_____

_____

_____

_____

_____

_____

_____

_____

Chapter 6: Profit

"Do well [financially] by doing good [helping others]"
–Benjamin Franklin

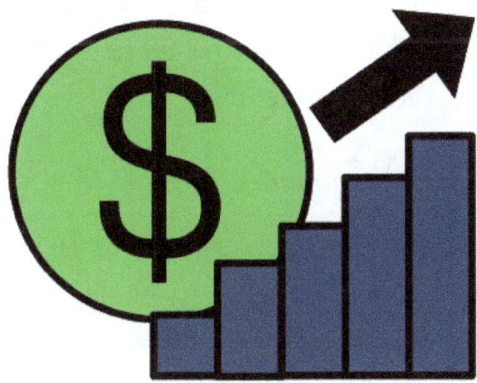

Description: Can Your Wheels Turn a Profit?

Turning a profit is what keeps the wheels rolling. Having multiple streams of income is critical in case one stream runs dry. As the saying goes, sometimes you have to take what you can get until you get what you want. What you want might be that dream position that aligns properly, but it may not be available right now. That is why you might have to earn extra income by working as a taxi, Uber, or private transportation driver. After all, money does not grow on trees, and bills need to be paid now. In the meantime, look for ways to work profitably in your desired field while solving real problems. Whether it's a temporary side hustle or your dream career, you need to figure out how to monetize your knowledge and skills to make a profit. We're talking about creating sustainable, credible income by solving real problems.

You should work to live, not live to work. Therefore, seek a mutually beneficial profession that connects with your Personality, Purpose, and Passion.

After that, pour your dedicated time and energy into your work. Remember the lessons from the story of "The Tortoise and the Hare," especially "Slow and steady wins the race." In this context, "slow" doesn't mean lazy and sluggish. Slow and unsteady will produce poor and late results. Fast and steady will produce stressful results. Slow and steady will produce balanced and consistent results.

Financial Literacy and Economic Opportunities

If your expenses consistently exceed your income, it can lead to financial trouble as you spend more than you earn and likely accumulate debt or drain your savings. Implement financial literacy practices such as creating and using a budget. "A budget is telling your money where to go instead of wondering where it went, helping you take control of your finances rather than being surprised by your spending."[69] It's also important to save and invest wisely. "Do not save what is left after spending; instead spend what is left after saving to ensure long-term financial stability."[70]

Understanding the difference between assets and liabilities is crucial. "An asset puts money in your pocket. A liability takes money out of your pocket."[71] Avoid high-interest debt like it's a disease, as it can severely damage your financial health. Save for a rainy day by maintaining an

---

[69] Ramsey, *The Money Answer Book*, 15.
[70] Lowenstein, *Buffett*.
[71] Kiyosaki, *Rich Dad Poor Dad*.

emergency fund of three to six months' worth of living expenses in cash. This financial cushion will prove invaluable if you lose your job or face unexpected costs. Galloway states, "The definition of 'rich' is having passive income greater than your burn. My dad and his wife receive about $50,000 a year from dividends, pension, and Social Security, and spend $40,000 a year. They are rich."[72] I assume some would want to have more money than that, but the point is that their *passive* income is more than their spending. Therefore, they're rich and not drowning in debt. Those financial decisions are multiple clutch moves over time.

"Compound interest is the eighth wonder of the world. He who understands it, earns it ... he who doesn't ... pays it" (attributed to Albert Einstein). Compound interest is the process of earning interest not only on your original investment (the principal), but also on the interest that has already been added to it. Pursue passive income, which is money you earn with little to no active involvement, such as through dividends from stocks or rental income from property. That way, money can drip into your account even while you're sleeping. Books such as *The Millionaire Next Door* and *The Psychology of Money* can improve your financial literacy.

Think about inventions or ways to sell or license your future product. For example, Bombas is one of the most successful companies to have appeared on Shark Tank. Bombas offers comfortable, high-quality socks with a "one for one" donation model, meaning that for every pair sold, one is donated to the homeless. It has grown into a major multimillion-dollar apparel brand.

Engaging in criminal activities for financial gain is discouraged because it's unethical and because the long arm of the law stretches far. However, there are notable examples of those who, after legal conviction, turned unethical or illegal activity into legitimate profit-making businesses. Kevin Mitnick was a hacker who became infamous in the 1990s for his unauthorized access

---

[72] Galloway, *Algebra of Happiness.*

to numerous computer networks. He was dubbed the "most wanted" computer hacker in the US. In 1999, Mitnick pleaded guilty to wire fraud and computer fraud charges and was sentenced to five years in prison. He was released in 2000 and would come to use his knowledge to train people to find data threats and computer crimes. Eventually, he was recognized as a respected cybersecurity consultant, author, and public speaker.

Don't forget to give back. One of the benefits of earning money is having the means to help others so they may one day continue to "pay it forward." Think about how and why we have libraries, nonprofits, and programs for neighbors in need. Maybe you've been able to use a service with no charge. Consider donating to at least one reputable charity in your local community.

The Internet Killed the Video Store

Internet Killed the Video Store is a documentary that explores the rise and fall of the video rental industry. David Cook was a software engineer making databases for oil and gas companies. Cook personally experienced problems with renting videos, two of which were the lack of an efficient database for finding movies and high fees for late returns.

Eventually, David created his own database of VHS movies and founded Blockbuster, a franchise of multiple physical stores. Cook left Blockbuster in 1987, two years after the company's founding. He sold a controlling stake to a group of investors, including Wayne Huizenga, for $18.5 million.

Netflix was started by Reed Hastings and Marc Randolph in 1997. The idea came about because Hastings was frustrated with paying late fees for rented movies. In 2010, Blockbuster filed for Chapter 11 bankruptcy due to declining sales and competition from Netflix, Redbox, and digital streaming.

Netflix initially adopted a DVD rental-by-mail model, offering a subscription service where customers could rent a DVD online, have it delivered to their homes, and then return the DVD by mail when they were done with it with no late fees. By offering a more convenient and customer-friendly service, Netflix quickly gained popularity and completely differentiated itself from traditional video rental stores.

As the internet improved, Netflix began transitioning into the streaming market. They quickly offered streaming of movies and TV shows online, eliminating the need for physical DVDs.

Netflix's subscription model, where customers pay a flat fee for unlimited streaming, provides consistent revenue streams. It also encourages more users to sign up for the membership, as they can consume as much content as they want without worrying about additional charges.

Another of Netflix's key strategies for sustaining growth and becoming profitable has been to invest in exclusive content as well as producing their own original shows and movies.[73]

Sustainable Profit

The Total Money Makeover is a personal finance book by Dave Ramsey provides a practical step-by-step approach to personal finance that can be highly beneficial for anyone looking to make a profit, whether through wisely managing money or growing wealth over time. The main concern is that the book doesn't focus on building a strong credit score which is important.

Entrepreneurs and companies should strive for a balanced approach to running their business, with the goal of sustainable profit, which is the result of making a purpose-based profit. In a *Forbes* article on sustainability and profitability, Turletti states, "Companies should address the needs of society and the improvement of the environment in a convergent manner through profitable projects that provide the air that companies need to live

---

[73] Lopez, *Internet Killed the Video Store.*

(profits) as well as the non-economic benefits they can generate to positively impact people and the planet at a steady pace."[74]

The United States of America is known for creativity, innovation, and profit generation. That reputation needs to continue, but sustainable profit should be emphasized also. "Sustainable profit" refers to profits generated through ethical practices, environmental stewardship, and social responsibility. This ensures long-term viability and minimal negative impact on society and on the planet. That approach can also minimize human exploitation and greed. Everybody wins: businesses, people, and society in general.

Different businesses and countries can learn from each other. For example, *Dorfwettbewerbe* (village competitions) and *konstruktiver Wettbewerb* (constructive competition) are two German concepts that play an important role in fostering community engagement, environmental sustainability, and profitability. These initiatives promote collaboration and innovation while maintaining a focus on sustainability.

Dorfwettbewerbe encourages local villages to improve their environmental practices through friendly competition, while *konstruktiver Wettbewerb* drives innovation in sectors like renewable energy, sustainable construction, and waste management. Both concepts combine competition with cooperation, resulting in a strong push toward greener, more sustainable practices across the country.

A Native American proverb wisely states, "Take only what you need and leave the land as you found it." While it may not always be possible to leave the land exactly as it was, that mindset fosters sustainability, long-term value creation, and decision-making guided by both the head and the heart. Making decisions based solely on rigid logic can lead to rapid short-term profits but often creates a cold and resentful "rat race" environment for

---

[74] Turletti, "Sustainability and Profitability."

employees and customers over time. Conversely, relying purely on emotion can cultivate empathy and creativity but may result in long-term instability and uncertainty. That's why a balanced approach that combines rational analysis with emotional intelligence is essential for sustainable success and a healthy organizational culture.

Effective Leadership for Sustainability

Many aspiring startup and small business owners often wear multiple hats out of necessity, especially due to limited staffing. Most commonly, they juggle the roles of leader and manager, guiding the team, and managing daily operations all at once. While these responsibilities often overlap, each has its own distinct focus and demands.

Entrepreneurs, as leaders, are responsible for guiding and motivating the team, setting a clear vision, and fostering a positive work culture. At the same time, entrepreneurs, as managers, must manage processes, execution, and systems, ensuring deadlines, budgets, and quality standards are met. Simultaneously, they oversee essential business operations like finances, marketing, and client relations to keep the company running smoothly and sustainably. Keep in mind that a "strong" or "tough" leader is not necessarily an effective leader. Figure 6.1 shows the distinctions of an effective leader as an acronym: LEADER. No leader is flawless, including those listed below, but they're able to demonstrate some or all of these timeless and universal leadership distinctions that can be transferred to any industry.

Figure 6.1. Distinctions of a LEADER

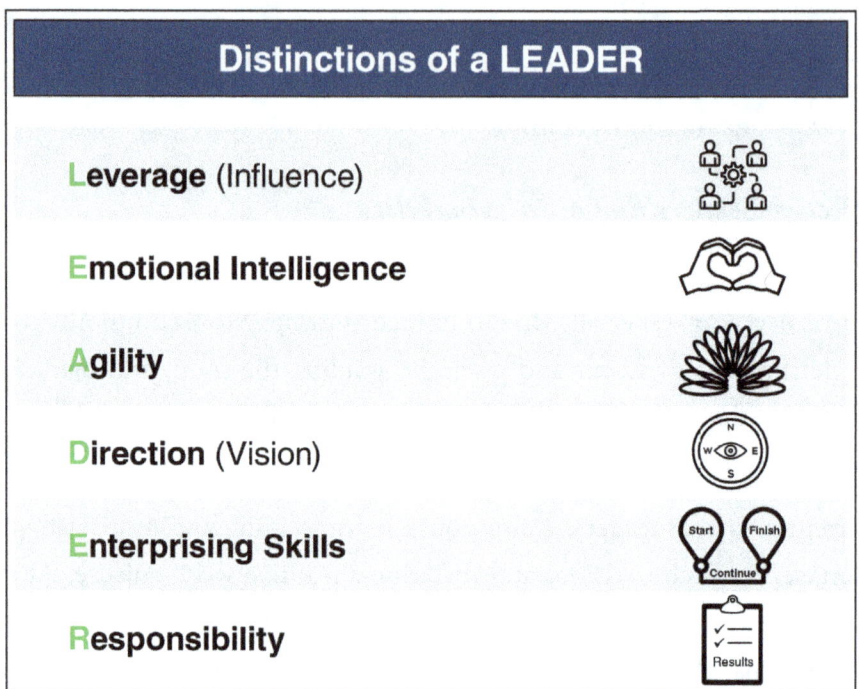

L is for leverage. That's a form of **influence**. "Leadership is influence."[75] Therefore, an influencer (not necessarily a social media influencer) is a leader who can lead positively or negatively. Influential leaders can directly or indirectly turn the gears that motivate people. That characteristic is also seen in servant leaders. In *Hacksaw Ridge* (2016),[76] the lead character Desmond Doss, portrayed by Andrew Garfield, exemplifies influence and servant leadership through his unwavering commitment to serving others above himself. This is the opposite of transactional leadership, which is more about a give-and-take or pay-to-play mentality. Initially, some made fun of Doss's beliefs and called him a coward. Despite refusing to carry a weapon, Doss courageously serves as a medic, repeatedly risking his life to save wounded soldiers. Desmond Doss was a real person, and for his

---

[75] Maxwell, *Developing the Leader Within You.*
[76] Gibson, dir.

bravery at the Battle of Okinawa, he became the first conscientious objector to receive the Medal of Honor.

E is for emotional intelligence (EI). EI is "your ability to recognize and understand emotions in yourself and others, and your ability to use this awareness to manage your behavior and relationships."[77] Nelson Mandela was known for being someone with a high level of EI. He became president of South Africa after serving twenty-seven years in prison. Mandela was portrayed in the movie *Invictus* by Morgan Freeman.[78] In the movie, various people on different occasions urged Mandela to seek revenge, but he made baffling statements in response, such as "Forgiveness liberates the soul" and "They are our partners in democracy" and "I know all the things they denied us, but this is no time for petty revenge." Mandela used that humble but strong approach, along with songs and rugby, to foster reconciliation and unity. Before incarceration, Mandela was an amateur boxer and an attorney. He was a strategic fighter who knew when to punch and when to pull the punch. As a leader and a politician, Mandela knew that in order for a bird to fly, it needs the balance of both wings: the left wing and the right wing.

A is for agility. Effective leaders are flexible like a slinky. That doesn't mean that they're spineless. That means sometimes the leadership approach is tough when it comes to requirements and sometimes it's flexible with options. "The best leaders don't know just one style of leadership—they're skilled at several, and have the flexibility to switch between styles as the circumstances dictate."[79] Goleman believes that effective leaders can switch appropriately between four leadership styles: authoritative (visionary), affiliative, democratic, and coaching.

---

[77] Bradberry and Greaves, *Emotional Intelligence 2.0.*
[78] Eastwood, dir.
[79] Goleman, "Leadership that Gets Results."

Warren Buffett was born into a middle-class family in the United States and went on to become an entrepreneur, investor, and billionaire philanthropist. He effectively demonstrates agile leadership by shifting between the four key leadership styles to suit different situations. As an **authoritative (visionary)** leader, Buffett sets a clear long-term vision focused on sustainable value creation and disciplined decision-making. His **affiliative** style is evident in the strong, trust-based relationships he builds with managers and stakeholders, emphasizing loyalty. Through a **democratic** approach, Buffett values input from his teams, granting autonomy to leaders within Berkshire Hathaway and encouraging decentralized decision-making. Finally, his **coaching** style is reflected in his commitment to mentoring executives and promoting learning through experience and patience.

Buffett pledged to donate most of his wealth to charitable causes and expressed that the super-rich, like him, should pay higher taxes. "To whom much is given, from him much will be required" (Luke 12:48). Buffett stated "While the poor and middle-class fight for us in Afghanistan, and while most Americans struggle to make ends meet, we mega-rich continue to get our extraordinary tax breaks."[80]

D is for direction (vision). Vision is a clear mental picture of a preferable future. Visionary leaders are skilled at painting the picture on the canvas of people's minds. You're able to **see** what they're saying. Favio Chávez, the creator of the Recycled Orchestra of Cateura (sometimes called the Landfill Orchestra), is a visionary leader because he transformed a community's waste into a source of hope, creativity, and opportunity.[81] Cateura is a Paraguayan slum built on a landfill, but Chávez saw beyond the poverty and trash. He envisioned a way to empower local youth through music by building instruments out of discarded materials, giving children a chance to develop their talents and change their lives. His leadership is visionary because he combined environmental sustainability,

---

[80] Politico, "Buffett: I beg you to raise my taxes."
[81] Allgood and Townsly, dirs. *Landfill Harmonic.*

social innovation, and cultural enrichment into a movement. Chávez's work not only created a world-renowned orchestra, it inspired global conversations about resilience, creativity, and the power of education to transform people and communities.

E is for enterprising skills. Leaders with this distinction start, continue, and finish their tasks. They are focused, consistent, and relentless like champion MMA fighters. Roy O. Disney turned the creative vision of his brother Walt into concrete results through persistence, strategic thinking, and a strong sense of responsibility. As cofounder of the Disney Brothers Studio in 1923, he provided the financial and managerial backbone that allowed Walt's ideas to flourish. While Walt created, Roy secured funding, negotiated deals, and kept the company stable through crises like the Great Depression and wartime struggles. After Walt's death in 1966, Roy came out of retirement to fulfill his brother's unfinished dream of building Walt Disney World. He personally oversaw the massive project to completion, ensuring its successful opening in 1971 and naming it in honor of Walt. Roy's ability to start, sustain, and finish complex tasks proves his quiet but powerful leadership was crucial to Disney's enduring success.

R is for responsibility. Every country has some level of corruption, but Alexei Navalny believed that with authority comes responsibility and accountability. As a Russian-born lawyer and political activist, he demonstrated strong responsibility as a leader by taking personal ownership of his fight against corruption. Despite being attacked multiple times, poisoned, and imprisoned on several occasions, Navalny remained steadfast in his mission. He openly stated that he was not afraid to die for his cause, displaying remarkable courage and commitment. His leadership drew massive crowds, tens of thousands of protesters, reflecting both his influence and the trust people placed in him. Navalny's actions showed that true leadership means accepting responsibility not only for oneself, but also for a larger cause and the people it serves. His family supported his efforts. Responsible leaders are not fault-finders who shift blame. In

February 2024, he died in prison at the age of 47. At the end of one documentary about him,[82] he is shown quoting a statement commonly attributed to Edmund Burke: "The only thing necessary for the triumph of evil is for good men to do nothing."

The Business Model Canvas for Profitability

As a leader, the entrepreneur can use the Business Model Canvas to promote sustainable profit. The Business Model Canvas is a strategic management tool used to visually outline and develop a business idea or existing business model. It was created by Alexander Osterwalder and is widely used by entrepreneurs, startups, and corporations to understand how a company creates, delivers, and captures value. By using the Business Model Canvas, entrepreneurs can gain a broad view of their operations and understand how they're really doing. This includes identifying which parts of the business are performing well, which are underperforming, and where value is being created or lost. With these insights, owners can make informed decisions rather than relying on guesswork.

Business owners need to GARD their data. That is, they must Gather, Analyze, Report, and Decide what actions to take based on the data. Then, they must implement strategies that enhance efficiency, reduce costs, improve customer satisfaction, and optimize revenue generation. For example, businesses can GARD the Return on Engagement (ROE) key performance indicator to boost customer satisfaction. The clarity and focus provided by the Business Model Canvas help companies identify areas for improvement, capitalize on opportunities, and minimize risks, ultimately leading to sustained profitability.

---

[82] Roher, dir., *Navalny.*

Management and Teamwork for Sustainability

"If you want to go fast, go alone. If you want to go far, go together" (African proverb). Many business owners believe that if something has to be done, they have to do it themselves, but that is not sustainable.

It's true that some things need to be done by the owner, but other tasks need to be delegated. In the animated movie *Cars*, Strip "The King" Weathers tells Lightning McQueen, "This ain't a one-man deal, kid. You need to wise up and get yourself a good crew chief and a good team. You ain't gonna win unless you got good folks behind you."[83]

This moment is significant because it marks a turning point for Lightning McQueen. Up to that point, he believed raw talent and individualism were enough to win. The King, a wise and experienced racer, reminds him that true success comes from collaboration, humility, and support, something Lightning eventually learns and embraces.

It also reflects real-life racing culture, where behind every champion driver is a team of mechanics, strategists, and mentors who make it all possible. This highlights the importance of relationships, teamwork, and the often-unseen forces that drive success, an idea closely tied to team-building and organizational psychology. Meaningful relationships are essential, as "rules without relationship leads to rebellion."[84] The film *F1* includes examples of relationship-building, as well as teamwork and mentoring. Brad Pitt's character, Sonny Hayes, is portrayed at times as a renegade, but he also serves as a mentor to rookie Joshua Pearce (Damson Idris), teaching him the value of collaboration.

Bruce W. Tuckman was an American psychologist who developed his own model of group development. It outlines four stages that teams go through to achieve high performance: forming, storming, norming, and performing. Similarly, author Patrick Lencioni[85] identified five dysfunctions of a team that

---

[83] Lasseter and Ranft, dirs. *Cars*.
[84] McDowell, "Rules without relationship."
[85] *The Five Dysfunctions of a Team.*

hinder effective teamwork: absence of trust, fear of conflict, lack of commitment, avoidance of accountability, and inattention to results.

Below is an abbreviated synthesis of Tuckman's model, Lencioni's model, and relevant scenes from Marvel's *Avengers: Age of Ultron*.

1. Forming: Group members meet.

In the early moments of *Avengers*, there is uncertainty as they try to understand their roles within the team. Nick Fury (Samuel Jackson) says, "There was an idea … to bring together a group of remarkable people, to see if we could become something more…"[86]

Lencioni's application: Build trust.

2. Storming: Conflict happens.

Captain America and Iron Man clash over how to approach the ongoing threats and Ultron's plan. Captain America (Steve Rogers) says: "Back off!" Tony Stark (Iron Man) responds: "I'm starting to want you to make me."[87]

Lencioni's application: Resolve conflict.

3. Norming: Resolution occurs and team normalizes.

The Avengers begin to understand each other's differences and strengths and work together more efficiently. While speaking about Loki, the antagonist, Iron Man demonstrates team unity when he tells Captain America that Loki "knows he has to take *us* out to win."[88]

Lencioni's application: Achieve commitment and embrace accountability

4. Performing: Team performs at a high caliber.

The team functions at its highest level during the final battle in *Age of Ultron*. Captain America is directing the team and turns to Natasha: "You and me, we stay here on the ground, keep the fighting here. And Hulk: Smash!"[89]

---

[86] Whedon, dir., *Avengers: Age of Ultron*.

[87] *Avengers: Age of Ultron*.

[88] *Avengers: Age of Ultron*.

[89] *Avengers: Age of Ultron*.

Lencioni's application: Focus on results.

Project Management for Profitability

Project managers lead the team and manage the project. Those are two different skill sets. Leading requires soft skills and managing requires hard skills. A "project" here is defined as a temporary endeavor undertaken to create a unique product, service, or result.[90] Therefore, managing a project is different than ongoing business operations such as accounting tasks.

Project managers have to PLOM the constraints of a project: Plan, Lead, Organize, and Monitor, which is displayed in Figure 6.2.

Figure 6.2. Project Managers PLOM

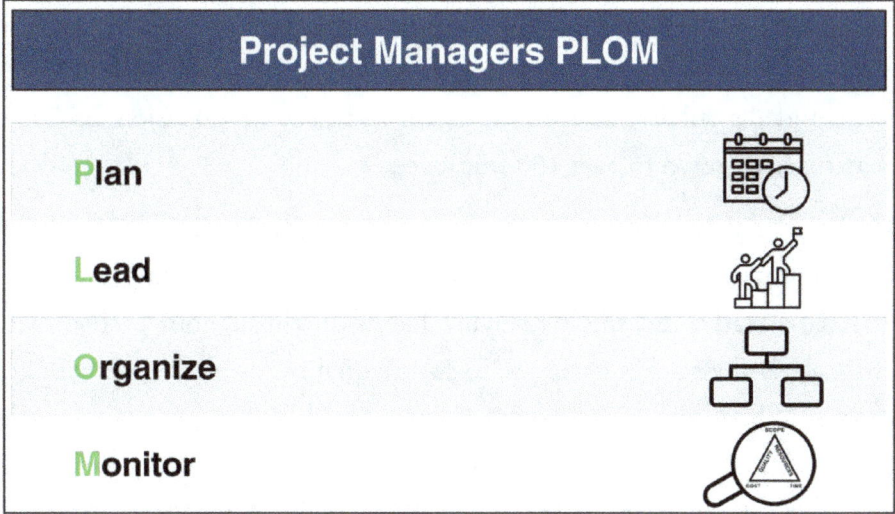

Zaha Hadid was a visionary architect who effectively PLOMed numerous projects throughout her career.

Plan: A plan contains a series of steps and a strategy designed to achieve specific goals. Hadid exemplified this through her careful project planning,

---

[90] Project Management Institute, *A Guide to the Project Management Body of Knowledge.*

developing bold yet practical design strategies. For the London Aquatics Centre for the 2012 Olympics, she collaborated early with engineers and planners to ensure her fluid vision was both achievable and structurally sound.

Lead: Sometimes leading people is like trying to get ten cats to walk in a straight line. Regardless, your leadership skills can be improved with practice over time. Hadid was the founder of her firm and she led by example. She championed bold, unconventional concepts and empowered her team to think beyond traditional design constraints, despite external skepticism.

Organize: Either organize or agonize. Many times, we agonize because we're disorganized. Have a method to your madness that works for you. Hadid did this by managing complex projects like the MAXXI Museum in Rome and the Guangzhou Opera House, where she led multidisciplinary teams and aligned diverse professionals around a common vision. By 2015, her firm had grown to over 400 employees.

Monitor: You have to monitor or track the cost (budget), time (schedule), scope (all required work), quality, and resources (labor, equipment, and material). Hadid did this by staying hands-on throughout each project phase, carefully tracking progress to ensure quality and alignment with her vision. While she wasn't directly responsible for managing total construction costs or detailed scheduling in the traditional project management sense, she collaborated closely with teams to ensure that design integrity was maintained. Her consistent oversight ensured that each project met both functional demands and artistic goals, earning her global recognition and prestigious awards like the Pritzker Prize and RIBA Gold Medal in 2016.

Elizabeth Harrin's Rebel's Guide to Project Management is a good start for project management resources.

Quality Management for Sustainability

In the context of quality improvement, practice Kaizen, which emphasizes continuous improvement through small, incremental changes that can be applied to any project or industry. This approach aligns seamlessly with the Plan-Do-Check-Act (PDCA) cycle, providing a structured methodology for implementing and evaluating improvements.

PDCA is a four-step iterative method used for continuous improvement in business processes, products, or services. Developed by Walter A. Shewhart and popularized by Dr. W. Edwards Deming in the 1950s, it is also known as the Deming Wheel. The following is a basic example of using this method to build or improve a *website*.

Plan: Identify an opportunity for improvement and plan a change. *Define clear goals, e.g., increase user engagement by improving site navigation. "Plan" includes drafting a sitemap and wireframes, and identifying KPIs.*

Do: Implement the change on a small scale. *Build a basic prototype of the new navigation structure and launch it for a small set of users or internal testing.*

Check: Evaluate the results of the change. *Analyze the test results. Compare bounce rates and pages per session; gather user feedback.*

Act: If the change was successful, standardize the new process. If not, identify what went wrong and begin the cycle again with a new plan. *If metrics improved, roll out the new navigation across the live site. If not, refine the design and repeat the cycle.*

Erik B. and Rakim Got "Paid in Full"

The song "Paid in Full" indirectly teaches valuable lessons about financial independence and making a profit. It's not partial or minimal payment; it's full payment.

According to Rakim, "You try to inspire people, you know what I mean? It's, like, putting the power in the listener's hands, letting them know they got it. The 'Paid in Full' song is actually the same thing: Letting everybody know, get [their] business together."[91]

Based on that statement and the song's lyrics, that might have been part of Rakim's professional goal: To become financially stable and encourage others to do the same.

In "Paid in Full," Rakim rhymes: "Me and Eric B. and a nice big plate of fish, which is my favorite dish."[92]

Rakim's favorite dish might represent some of the pleasantries that he wants to maintain and acquire (meaningful relationships and assets). That might be one of his implicit personal goals.

However, achieving his personal goals means making enough money to afford them with financial independence.

In addition, he is able to do what he loves, which is making music, and get paid for it. That's how to have fun while getting it done. Having a lot of money isn't the ultimate goal; rather, it's a tool to build lasting wealth and create a more balanced life—one that includes quality time, health, financial stability, peace of mind, and personal freedom.

---

[91] Mao, "Rakim."
[92] Eric B. & Rakim, "Paid in Full."

Instructions: Accelerate For Growth

You'll create your profit guiding principle by answering some questions. The answer to the first question will serve as your fourth foundational goal.

Example

GOAL IV

How can you profit while executing your plan to solve the problem with your Personality, Purpose, and Passion? (Sustainability)

I will prioritize a work-life balance and network to secure freelance opportunities and career advancements that are socially responsible, supporting both sustainability and my vision.

Why is your solution (product, service, or idea) desirable, viable, and feasible? (Marketability)

My service-based solution is marketable because PM principles are timeless, universal, and transferable, aligning with industry standards and KPIs including customer satisfaction.

Assemble

Fill in the blanks in the GPS Map with one brief sentence each.

GOAL IV

How can you profit while executing your plan to solve the problem with your Personality, Purpose, and Passion? (Sustainability)

_____

_____

Why is your solution (product, service, or idea) desirable, viable, and feasible? (Marketability)

_____

_____

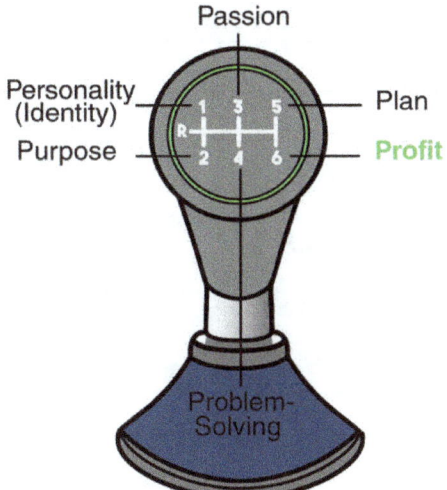

Practice: Reinforce Your Profit GPS

Shift: Symbolically shift into the Profit GPS sixth gear.

Practice: Create a budget and track your spending. Alternatively, engage in a game like *Power Grid*, which emphasizes resource management and economic growth.

Describe and/or draw your own ways of how you can (and will) practice your Profit GPS.

Discuss your ideas with select people to reinforce what you've completed so far.

_____

_____

_____

_____

_____

_____

_____

_____

Rest Stop 2: Professional Goals Summary

Put your car in park to relax and reflect. In a sense, you've sorted and connected your Professional GPS puzzle pieces. That means the second half of your treasure map is done!

To recap, in order to solve a problem, you first have to acknowledge that the problem exists. It's important to consider how you can help others in your profession. A practical way to do this is by helping other people, or other companies, solve problems.

That means you must plan the work and then work the plan, adjusting as needed. Don't aim for perfection. Just strive for progress through iteration. Having multiple streams of income is critical in case one stream runs dry. Entrepreneurs and companies should work toward a balanced approach to running their business, where the goal is sustainable profit.

Paired Goals Introduction

"Work-life balance is achieved when equilibrium between work and other life domains is viable and sustainable."
–Vanda Marques and Gregory Berry

Your paired goals are where your personal and professional goals are bridged together. By completing your GPS Map, you've paired your personal (life) goals with your professional (work) goals. The bridge provides access to both sides.

Now it's time to put these combined principles into active practice, which is the only way to actually achieve your goals.

You can't learn to drive, especially a manual transmission, in a parked car! Now, you're able to shift any of the six gears to visit and spend the necessary time at those corresponding locations.

Progress often comes through trial, error, and adjustment, so don't be afraid to stall, skid or make other mistakes along the way. What matters most is that you keep learning and moving forward. As you gain momentum, navigating between your personal and professional goals will start to feel more natural, like cruising on a well-maintained road. Keep your map in sight, check your mirrors, and enjoy the ride toward your destination.

The Implied GPS For Claude Monet

Although he probably didn't call it as such, it seems like Claude Monet, a pioneering French painter, integrated the GPS principles to pair his personal life goals and professional work goals. His home and garden became central to his artistic process, serving as both sanctuary and studio. Gustave Geffroy, an art critic, novelist, and good friend of Monet, gives us a glimpse into his personality: "The **person** who designed and laid out this magnificent little domestic world is a great artist not only when creating paintings but also when creating an enjoyable setting for his life."[93] He enjoyed capturing the transient beauty of nature, which aligned with his **purpose** of conveying the passing qualities of light, color, and the atmosphere. This dedication fueled his **passion** for what is called *plein-air* painting, which means going outdoors and painting in natural light and surroundings instead of working under artificial conditions inside a studio.

Monet's **problem-solving** abilities were evident in his innovative approach to art and commerce. Faced with initial rejection from traditional art institutions, he sought alternative avenues to showcase his work and turned to collaborating with fellow artists. This allowed Monet to play a pivotal role in **planning** independent exhibitions, notably the first Impressionist exhibition in 1874. This initiative not only provided a platform for his own art but established a new artistic movement.

---

[93] Geffroy, "Quotes."

Despite personal hardships such as depression, the deaths of loved ones, and financial struggles in his early career, Monet found peace in creating beauty from his natural, everyday environment.

Financially, Monet's strategic partnerships and marketing acumen contributed to his **profitability**. His collaboration with art dealer Paul Durand-Ruel was instrumental. Durand-Ruel's commitment to promoting Monet's work expanded his reach to international collectors, ensuring financial stability and broader recognition.

Beyond his personal achievements, Monet's legacy includes mentoring emerging artists and sharing his own techniques and insights, thus fostering the growth of Impressionism. Today, Monet's works continue to be employed in art therapy as an aid to relaxation and mindfulness, demonstrating the enduring impact of his integrated approach to both art and life.

Skills and Knowledge Check

Knowledge is about knowing; skills are about doing. Both are essential for performance improvement and SKAN development. Your combined GPS should flow from your head (the thinker) to your heart (the feeler) to your hands (the doer).

The core questions in Chart A, the Skills and Knowledge Check, are designed to consistently remind, challenge, and motivate you to use your GPS Map to relentlessly pursue your paired goals. Try to answer as many questions from the chart as you can without referring to your previous answers.

How many of the chapter Reinforcement Points have you started or completed? For example, have you created and used your budget? Periodically revisit this chart as you continue your journey.

Chart A. Skills and Knowledge Check

Personal Life Goals		Professional Work Goals
Personality • Who are you? (Identity) • Where are you from? (History)	⬅➡	**Problem-solving** • What customer-based problem can you solve with your personality, purpose, and passion? (Creativity) • Why do you want to solve this problem? (Professional Purpose - Why?) • What's the value proposition (benefits) for the potential customers if you fix the problem? (Mutual Satisfaction)
Purpose • Why are you here? (Utility) • What stage of life are you in now? (Reality) • Where are you going? (Vision and Destiny)		**Plan** • What's your executable plan to solve the problem with your personality, purpose, and passion? (Mission) • How, when, and where can/will you solve the problem? (Strategy)
Passion • What do you value (find worth in and believe in)? (Appreciation) • What do you really enjoy doing for fun? (Motivation) • What's your preferred future occupation? (Ambition)		**Profit** • How can you profit while executing your plan to solve the problem with your personality, purpose, and passion? (Sustainability) • Why is your solution (product, service, or idea) desirable, viable, and feasible? (Marketability)

The Persistence Multi-Tool Preview

If there was a seventh GPS, it would be *Persistence*. Persistence means sticking with something and not giving up until you have achieved it. Practicing with Persistence is essential. Specifically, we call this the Persistence Multi-tool. It's critical for you to use the Persistence Multi-tool to follow through with your GPS Map in order to complete your personal and professional goals.

The Persistence Multi-tool consists of these individual tools or phases: Define, Design, Develop & Execute, Detect, Deliver, and Debrief.

More details are in a chart after the conclusion.

Don't think you're going to plant the seed today and pick the fruit tomorrow. You'll need patience, and the plant will require consistent care and attention from you. Later, you can enjoy the fruit of your labor. Many people discover "overnight successes" on platforms like YouTube or TikTok, unaware that these individuals have often spent years perfecting their craft before achieving recognition. It took Dale Earnhardt twenty attempts over twenty years to win the Daytona 500 race.[94] This long

---

[94] Beaver, "Twenty-Five Years Later."

journey exemplifies how great achievement rarely arrives overnight; it's built through perseverance and unwavering commitment.

Persistence is one of the parts of "Following Through" as outlined in the book *Finish What You Start* by Peter Hollins, who states, "Following through can be said to be composed of four parts: Focus, Self-Discipline, Action, and **Persistence**."[95] It's not just about working hard once, but about continuing to show up and make progress even when it's difficult or progress feels slow. This steady commitment helps bridge the gap between intention and completion, turning goals into achievements through sustained action. You have two options: make excuses or make it happen. Let's make it happen!

Personal Life–Professional Work Balancing Tips

1. **Set Boundaries.** Clearly define work hours and personal time. Avoid taking work calls or checking messages during personal time to maintain a separation between work and home life. Digital nomads and remote workers must be especially mindful of this separation.

2. **Prioritize Tasks.** Use tools like to-do lists or planners to prioritize tasks. Focus on what is most important and delegate or postpone less critical tasks.

3. **Seek Flexible Work Arrangements.** If possible, consider flexible work hours or remote work options. This can help accommodate personal responsibilities and reduce commute times.

4. **Take Breaks.** Regular breaks during work hours can improve focus and productivity. Ensure you take time for short walks, relaxation, or hobbies to recharge.

---

[95] Hollins, *Finish What You Start.*

5. **Practice Time Management.** Implementing time management techniques like the Eisenhower Matrix, time blocking, and task batching can help to distribute your time more effectively.

6. **Reduce Procrastination.** "Don't put off for tomorrow what can be done today"—attributed to Benjamin Franklin.[96]

7. **Remember the Serenity Prayer.** "God grant me the serenity to accept the things I cannot change [e.g., people's behavior], courage to change the things I can [e.g., my reactions to their behavior], and wisdom to know the difference."[97]

---

[96] Franklin, *Poor Richard's Almanack.*
[97] Niebuhr, "Serenity Prayer."

Rest Stop 3: Paired Goals Summary

Having a GPS Map is one thing; following it with persistence is another. But reaching your goals is the ultimate achievement! Let your completed treasure map guide you on this quest. This journey requires consistent effort and a willingness to push through challenges. As Hollins emphasizes, "Following through is the more difficult path, but the benefits it can yield make the journey worth the struggle."[98] In other words, it's not enough to dream and plan. You must consistently act on the dream and the plan.

Building this kind of initiative and follow-through is deeply connected to the habits we form. Small, repeated actions over time can lead to substantial outcomes. James Clear, in his book *Atomic Habits*, states, "Habits are the compound interest of self-improvement. The same way that money multiplies through compound interest, the effects of your habits multiply as you repeat them."

This highlights the power of daily routines and behaviors in shaping long-term success. Even minor changes, when practiced consistently, can lead to profound personal growth and achievement!

---

[98] Hollins, *Finish What You Start*.

Thanks for Your Support!

Please pause to scan the QR code to leave a brief and open review.
Your words can help others.

Or input the URL below in your web browser.
https://bityl.co/Syb9

Chart B: GPS Puzzle

Below is the Paired GPS Puzzle Example That You Solved

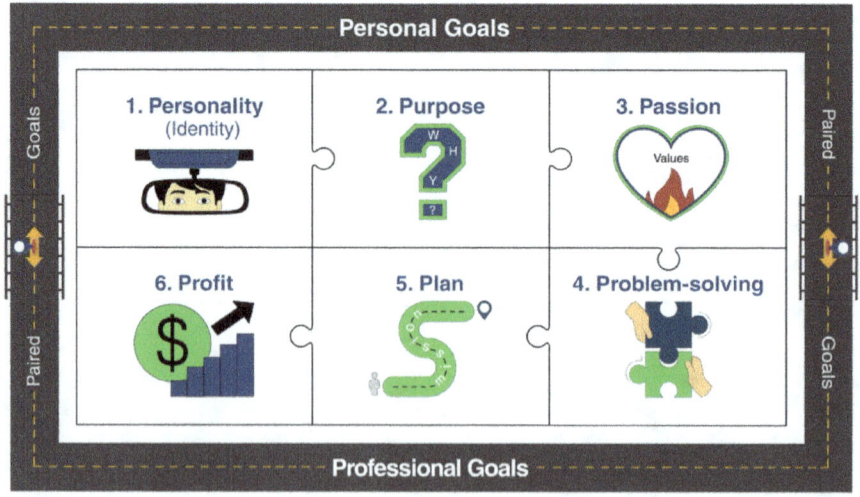

Conclusion: Finish Line

"Having a healthy work/life balance is [essential] …
to reach our business and personal goals."
–Dr. Travis G. Parry

The checkered flag is waving for you! Congratulations on symbolically bridging the gap between your personal and professional goals and making it across the finish line! A big high five to you, GPS Driver!

Later, you can refine your GPS Map if necessary. Then, continue realistically DAPing (Describing, Assembling, and Practicing) your GPS to achieve your integrated goals for a more balanced life.

It's customary to face roadblocks and feel tired along the road. During those times, sing along with Andy Grammer: "Gotta keep your head up!"[99] Make your clutch moves and let the journey continue!

---

[99] Grammer, "Keep Your Head Up."

The Persistence Multi-Tool:
The Journey Continues

Chart C

The Persistence Multi-Tool	
• "Following through is the powerful combination of focus, self-discipline, action, and **persistence**" (Hollins, 2018). • Below is a modified version of the EPD Life Cycle, adapted for the GPS Map and your Goals. • Each of the five phases serves as a **persistence** tool. • You've basically completed the GPS Map tasks (highlighted in grey below). • Now, execute with your Persistence Multi-Tool to achieve all your goals!	

Define	All GPS locations were defined and described
	All Goals were defined and described
Design	All GPS locations were assembled
	All Goals were assembled
Develop & Execute	All GPS locations were developed and symbolically activated
	All Goals were developed. The complete plan needs to be executed.
Detect (Test)	All GPS locations were practiced and symbolically tested
	All Goals need to be tested (e.g. realign if necessary)
Deliver	The GPS Map was delivered and can be modified as needed
	The Goals need to be **persistently** pursued for achievement.

The Interactive eLearning Experience
Test Drive Demo

Type the following link in your internet browser to access:

https://tinyurl.com/y962rdmv

Just in Case You Missed It,
Thanks for Your Support!

Please pause to scan the QR code and leave a brief and open review.

Your words can help others.

Or use the URL below.

https://bityl.co/Syb9

Optional Third-Party Resources

All readers, including Career Counselors, Educators, and L&D Trainers can use these resources to reinforce the GPS. There's a cost to access some of them.

MBTI Personality Type Assessment (self-quiz)

Finding Your Roots (TV series)

Born a Crime: Stories from a South African Childhood (book)

The Chronicles of Narnia (book series)

Soul (Disney & Pixar movie)

Little White Lie (documentary movie)

Gabriel Iglesias: Fluffy Stopped by Border Patrol (video)

De La Soul: "Me Myself and I" (music)

Casting Crowns: "Who Am I" (music)

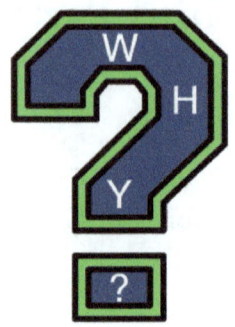

The Purpose Driven Life (book)

The Five Love Languages: Singles Edition (book)

The Concise Mastery (book)

The Sims (video game)

Coach Carter and *Hacksaw Ridge* (movies)

Andra Day: "Rise Up" (music)

U2: "I Still Haven't Found What I'm Looking For" (music)

The Live Your Values Deck (book)

Freedom Writers (movie)

Mindful Leadership: Emotional Intelligence Collection (book)

Landfill Harmonic and ESPN's *30 for 30* (documentary series)

Alicia Keys: "Underdog" and Marc Anthony: "Vivir Mi Vida" (music)

The Game of Life 2 (board and video game)

Finding Your Element: How to Discover Your Talents and Passions and Transform Your Life (book)

Value Proposition Design (book)

Creativity, Inc. (book)

GitHub Education (software)

Ninite (software)

Hidden Figures (movie)

Abstract: The Art of Design (TV series)

Minecraft and *Civilization* (video games)

Marvin Gaye: "What's Going On" (music)

Tracy Chapman: "Fast Car" (music)

Bob Marley: "So Much Trouble in the World" (music)

Tears For Fears: "Everybody Wants to Rule the World" (music)

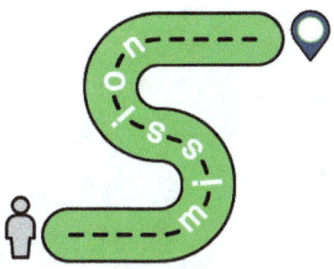

Developing the Leader Within You 2.0 (book)

The Fast Forward MBA in Project Management (book)

Interaction Design Foundation (website)

"What Is Personal Branding?" (article)

7 Days Out (TV series)

Fyre (documentary)

Pocket City 2 and *RollerCoaster Tycoon* (video games)

McFadden & Whitehead: "Ain't No Stoppin' Us Now" (music)

Jimmy Cliff: "You Can Get It if You Really Want" (music)

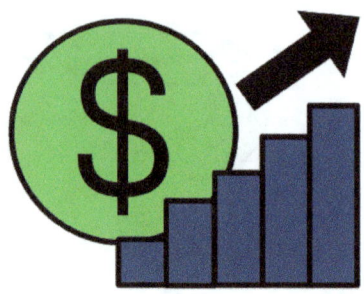

The Total Money Makeover (book)

The Business Model Canvas (book)

The Five Dysfunctions of a Team, Manga Edition (book)

The Mega-Brands That Built America (TV series)

The Profit (TV series)

SimCity BuildIt (video game)

Capsim (software)

Eric B. & Rakim: "Paid in Full" (music)

The Secret Structure of Great Talks (TED Talk)

Bibliography

ABC News. "Shania Twain Opens Up About Her Difficult Childhood, Heart-Wrenching Divorce, and Finding Love Again." *ABC News*, May 4, 2011. https://abcnews.go.com/Entertainment/shania-twain-opens-difficult-childhood-heart-wrenching-divorce/story?id=13529925.

Alawajee, Omar, and Jonathan Delafield-Butt. "Minecraft in Education Benefits Learning and Social Engagement." *International Journal of Game-Based Learning* 11, no. 4 (2021): 19–56. https://doi.org/10.4018/IJGBL.2021100102.

Allgood, Brad, and Graham Townsley, dirs. *Landfill Harmonic.* Meetai Films, 2015.

Ancestry. "John Lithgow Is Related to Clint Eastwood, Sally Field and WHO??" *Finding Your Roots*, June 25, 2023. Video, 4 min., 22 sec. https://youtu.be/ekBa4G9TIZ4?si=W1I7xuf4LUOAycoj.

Anthony, Marc. (2013). "Vivir Mi Vida." *3.0*. Sony Music Latin. Released July 23, 2013.

Beaver, Dan. "Twenty-Five Years Later, Dale Earnhardt's Daytona 500 Victory Still Stands the Test of Time." *NASCAR.com*, February 15, 2023. https://www.nascar.com/news-media/2023/02/15/dale-earnhardts-daytona-500-victory-still-resonates/.

Benjamin, C. L. *Dog Problems: A Professional Trainer's Guide to Preventing and Correcting Aggression.* Doubleday, 1981.

Bradberry, Travis, and Jean Greaves. *Emotional Intelligence 2.0.* TalentSmart, 2009.

Branje, Susan, Elizabeth L. de Moor, Jenna Spitzer, and Andrik I. Becht. "Dynamics of Identity Development in Adolescence: A Decade in Review." *Journal of Research on Adolescence* 31, no. 4 (2021): 908–927. https://doi.org/10.1111/jora.12678.

Brown, Brené. *Braving the Wilderness: The Quest for True Belonging and the Courage to Stand Alone.* Random House, 2017.

Brown, Brené. *The Gifts of Imperfection: Let Go of Who You Think You're Supposed to Be and Embrace Who You Are.* Hazelden Publishing, 2010.

Brown, Duane, ed. *Career Choice and Development.* 4th ed. Jossey-Bass, 2002.

Bulger, Carrie. "Work-Life Balance." In *Encyclopedia of Quality of Life and Well-Being Research*, edited by Filomena Maggino. Springer, 2024. https://doi.org/10.1007/978-3-031-17299-1_3270.

Campbell, Joseph. *A Joseph Campbell Companion: Reflections on the Art of Living (The Collected Works of Joseph Campbell).* Edited by Robert Walter and David Kudler. HarperCollins, 1991.

Canfield, Jack, and Janet Switzer. *The Success Principles: How to Get from Where You Are to Where You Want to Be.* 10th anniversary ed. William Morrow, 2015.

Clear, James. *Atomic Habits: An Easy & Proven Way to Build Good Habits & Break Bad Ones.* Avery, 2018.

Covey, Stephen R. *The 7 Habits of Highly Effective People.* 30th anniversary ed. Simon & Schuster, 2020.

D'Alessandro, Emily, Dana Jacobson, and Heather Spinelli. "How The Sims Grew from a Virtual Construction Game into a Cultural Phenomenon." *CBS News*, February 21, 2025. https://www.cbsnews.com/news/the-sims-25-years-cultural-phenomenon/.

Dalberg, John Emerich Edward, Lord Acton. *Historical Essays and Studies*, eds. Reginald Vere Laurence and John Neville Figgis. Macmillan, 1907.

Date, Hayato, dir. "Uzumaki Naruto!! 'Saishûkai.'" *Naruto Shippuden*, season 1, episode 479. TV Tokyo, 2016.

De La Soul. (2014, December 11). "De La Soul - Me Myself and I (With Intro) (Official Music Video)." WeAreDeLaSoul, YouTube, 3 min., 56 sec. https://youtu.be/zR9AlcgL6_0?si=jjathuSFUV7JMf37.

Docter, Pete, and Kemp Powers, dirs. *Soul*. Pixar Animation Studios and Walt Disney Pictures, 2020.

Duckworth, Angela. *Grit: The Power of Passion and Perseverance.* Scribner, 2018.

Eastwood, Clint, dir. *Invictus*. Spyglass Entertainment, 2009.

Edelman and Adobe. *2024 Creative AI Jobs Report.* Adobe, 2024.

Eggar, Robin. *Shania Twain: the Biography*. Gallery Books, 2005.

Eldrege, John. *Wild at Heart: Discovering the Secret of a Man's Soul*. Thomas Nelson, 2001.

Electronic Arts. *The Sims Mobile*. Released 2017. https://www.ea.com/games/the-sims/the-sims-mobile.

Eric B. & Rakim. (1987). "Paid in Full." *Paid in Full.* 4th & B'way Records. Released July 7, 1987.

Farri, Elisa, and Gabriele Rosani. *HBR Guide to Generative AI for Managers.* Harvard Business Review Press, 2025.

Franklin, Benjamin. *Poor Richard's Almanack*, edited by C. H. G. Van Buren. Printed for the author, 1757.

Friedman, Stewart D., and Jeffrey H. Greenhaus. *Work and Family: Allies or Enemies?* Oxford University Press, 2000.

Galloway, Scott. *The Algebra of Happiness: Notes on the Pursuit of Success, Love, and Meaning.* Portfolio, 2019.

Galloway, Scott, and Sean Illing, hosts. "Are Men Okay?" *The Prof G Pod with Scott Galloway*, podcast. Vox Media, December 17, 2024.

García, Héctor, & Francesc Miralles. *Ikigai: The Japanese Secret to a Long and Happy Life*. Penguin Life, 2017.

Garibaldi, Christina, & Jaime Harkin. (2025, March 5). "Shania Twain Gets Candid about Body Confidence, a Biopic and Turning 60: 'There Is No Other Me' (Exclusive)." *Us Weekly*, March 5, 2025. https://www.usmagazine.com/celebrity-news/news/shania-twain-gets-candid-body-confidence-biopic-and-turning-60-excl/.

Gaye, Marvin. (1971). "*What's Going On.*" *What's Going On*. Motown. Released May 21, 1971.

Geffroy, Gustave. (n.d.). "Quotes." *Fondation Monet*. Retrieved April 24, 2025, from https://fondation-monet.com/en/decouvrir/quotes/.

Gentry, Ric. "When Shooting Starts, He's Mr. Efficiency: Eastwood's Malpaso 'Family' Generally Does the Job On Time and Under

Budget." *Los Angeles Times*, May 21, 1989. https://www.latimes.com/archives/la-xpm-1989-05-21-ca-806-story.html.

George, Bob. *Classic Christianity: Life's Too Short to Miss the Real Thing.* Harvest House Publishers, 2010.

Gibson, Mel, dir. *Hacksaw Ridge.* Summit Entertainment, 2016.

Glassman, Charles F. *Brain Drain: The Breakthrough that Will Change Your Life*. RTS Publishing, 2009.

Goleman, Daniel. "Leadership that Gets Results." *Harvard Business Review*, March-April (2000).

Grammer, Andy. "Keep Your Head Up." *Andy Grammer*. S-Curve Records. Released June 14, 2011.

Greene, Robert. *Mastery*. Penguin Books, 2012.

Haines, Chrstine. "Experience of Transition from the Military for Combat Veterans Who Served after 9/11." *Archives of Physical Medicine and Rehabilitation* 106, no. 4 (2025): E152. https://doi.org/10.1016/j.apmr.2025.01.392.

Harvard Business Review, Russell Glass, Morra Aarons-Mele, Alyssa F. Westring, and Amantha Imber. *Boundaries, Priorities, and Finding Work-Life Balance.* Harvard Business Review Press, 2024.

Hehir, Jason, dir. *The Last Dance.* Netflix, 2020. https://www.netflix.com/title/80203144.

Helgeland, Brian, dir. *42*. Warner Bros. Pictures, 2013.

Hetherington, Tim, and Sebastian Junger, dirs. *Restrepo*. National Geographic Entertainment, 2010.

Hollins, Peter. *Finish What You Start: The Art of Following Through, Taking Action, Executing, & Self-Discipline (Live a Disciplined Life)*. CreateSpace Independent Publishing Platform, 2018.

Huxley, Aldous. *Proper Studies*. Chatto & Windus, 1927.

Iglesias, Gabriel. *I'm Not Fat ... I'm Fluffy*. Triage Entertainment, 2009.

Indeed Editorial Team, "What Is Personal Branding? (And How It Can Help You)." *Indeed*, January 28, 2025. https://www.indeed.com/career-advice/career-development/what-is-personal-branding.

Isaacson, Walter, ed. *A Benjamin Franklin Reader*. Simon & Schuster, 2005.

Judge, T. P., and R. Ilies. (2002). "Relationship of Personality to Performance Motivation: A Meta-Analytic Review." *Journal of Applied Psychology* 87, no. 4 (2002): 799–808. http://dx.doi.org/10.1037/0021-9010.87.4.797.

Jung, Carl, and Aniela Jaffé. *Memories, Dreams, Reflections*. Pantheon Books, 1963.

Keith, Clinton, and Grant Shonkwiler. *Creative Agility Tools: 100+ Tools for Creative Innovation and Teamwork*. Clinton Keith, 2018.

Kelley, Tom, and David Kelley. *Creative Confidence: Unleashing the Creative Potential Within Us All*. Crown Currency, 2013.

Kelly, Matthew. *Off Balance: Getting Beyond the Work-Life Balance Myth to Personal and Professional Satisfaction.* Hudson Street Press, 2011.

Kiyosaki, Robert T. *Rich Dad Poor Dad: What the Rich Teach Their Kids that the Poor and Middle Class Do Not!* Warner Books, 1997.

LaGravenese, Richard, dir. *Freedom Writers.* Paramount Pictures, 2007.

Lasseter, John, and Joe Ranft, dirs. *Cars.* Pixar Animation Studios and Walt Disney Pictures, 2006.

Lazenby, Roland. *Michael Jordan: The Life.* Back Bay Books, 2015.

Lencioni, Patrick. *The Five Dysfunctions of a Team: A Leadership Fable.* Jossey-Bass, 2002.

Lewis, John. 2012 Commencement Address at UConn School of Law. May 20, 2012. https://today.uconn.edu/2020/07/john-lewis-2012-commencement-address-uconn-school-law/.

Locke, Edwin A., and Gary P. Latham, eds. *New Developments in Goal Setting and Task Performance.* Routledge, 2013.

Lopez, Richard, dir. *The Mega-Brands that Built America.* Season 2, episode 2, "Internet Killed the Video Store." Aired May 5, 2024, on History. https://www.imdb.com/title/tt32052393/.

Lowenstein, Roger. *Buffett: The Making of an American Capitalist.* Simon & Schuster, 2005.

McDowell, Josh. "Rules without relationship leads to rebellion," *Josh McDowell Quotes, Quote.org,* accessed September 6, 2025, https://www.quote.org/quote/rules-without-relationship-leads-to-rebellion-1234

Mackay, Harvey. *Swim with the Sharks Without Being Eaten Alive: Outsell, Outmanage, Outmotivate, and Outnegotiate Your Competition.* William Morrow and Company, 1988.

Mao, Jeff "Chairman." (2013). "Rakim." *Red Bull Music Academy Lectures.* https://www.redbullmusicacademy.com/lectures/rakim-lecture.

Marcus, J. S. "A Monet Mentor's Moment." *Wall Street Journal*, March 18, 2016.

Marley, Bob. (1979). "Wake Up and Live." *Survival.* Island Records. Released October 2, 1979.

Marques, Vanda C., and Gregory R. Berry. "Enhancing Work-Life Balance Using a Resilience Framework." *Business and Society Review* 126, no. 3 (2021): 263–281. https://doi.org/10.1111/basr.12237.

Maxwell, John C. *Developing the Leader Within You 2.0.* HarperCollins, 2018.

Maxwell, John C. *The 15 Invaluable Laws of Growth.* Center Street, 2012.

Melfi, Theodore, dir. *Hidden Figures.* Fox 2000 Pictures, 2016.

Menon, Amrita. "Claude Monet: Painting Entrepreneurial Success with Brushstrokes of Innovation." *Medium* (blog), May 25, 2023. https://medium.com/@menonamrita2/claude-monet-painting-entrepreneurial-success-with-brushstrokes-of-innovation-c30c16ed7d19.

Microsoft and LinkedIn. *2024 Annual Work Trend Index.* https://news.microsoft.com/annual-wti-2024/.

Miranda, Lin-Manuel, composer. *Hamilton: Original Broadway Cast Recording.* Atlantic Recording Corporation. Released 2015.

Mojang Studios. *Minecraft.* Released 2011. https://www.minecraft.net/en-us.

Murden, Fiona. *Defining You: How to Profile Yourself and Unlock Your Full Potential.* 2nd ed. Nicholas Brealey, 2021.

Ngezahayo, Sim. *Essentials of Career Management for Language Professionals: A Blueprint for Mastering Your Career and Leading a Healthy Work-Life Balance.* Tellwell Talent, 2022.

Niebuhr, Reinhold. "Serenity Prayer." 1943.

Orwell, George. *Animal Farm.* Secker and Warburg, 1945.

Osterwalder, Alexander, Yves Pigneur, Gregory Bernarda, and Alan Smith. *Value Proposition Design: How to Create Products and Services Customers Want.* Wiley, 2014.

Parry, Travis Gregg. *Achieving Balance: The Make Time Method to Help Advisors Reach Business AND Personal Goals in an Overworked World.* Independently published, 2022.

Phelps, Michael, and Alan Abrahamson. *No Limits: The Will to Succeed.* Free Press, 2009.

Pinhas, Hannah. "Project Management Statistics: 45 Stats You Can't Ignore." *Workamajig*, September 19, 2022. https://www.workamajig.com/blog/project-management-statistics.

Pink, Daniel H. *Drive: The Surprising Truth about What Motivates Us.* Riverhead Books, 2011.

POLITICO Staff. (2011, August 15). *Buffett: I beg you to raise my taxes.* Politico. https://www.politico.com/story/2011/08/buffett-i-beg-you-to-raise-my-taxes-061370

Project Management Institute. *A Guide to the Project Management Body of Knowledge.* 7th ed. Project Management Institute, 2021.

Ramsey, Dave. *The Money Answer Book: Quick Answers for Your Everyday Financial Questions.* Thomas Nelson, 2010.

Ramsey, Dave. *The Total Money Makeover: A Proven Plan for Financial Fitness.* Thomas Nelson, 2013.

Robinson, Ken, and Lou Aronica. *Finding Your Element: How to Discover Your Talents and Passions and Transform Your Life.* Viking, 2013.

Roher, Daniel, dir. *Navalny.* CNN Films, 2022.

Rohn, Jim. *The Power of Ambition: Awakening the Powerful Force Within You.* Sound Wisdom, 2022.

Rosana, Anita, & Irfan Fauzi. (2024). "The Role of Digital Identity in the Age of Social Media: Literature Analysis on Self-Identity Construction and Online Social Interaction." *Journal of Social Science* 1, no. 4 (2024): 477–489. http://dx.doi.org/10.59613/a8yyff42.

Santayana, George. *The Life of Reason: Reason in Common Sense.* Vol. 1. Charles Scriber's Sons, 1905.

Sharma, Ekta, and Madhuri Jha. "Work-Life Balance: A Key to Positive Workplace Attitudes." *Indian Journal of Industrial Relations* 57, no. 1 (2021): 99–110.

Shaw, Nathan. *Work-Life Balance Hacks: Mindset Shifts and Habits for Succeeding at Work and Having a Life.* Independently published, 2025.

Shay, Jonathan. *Achilles in Vietnam: Combat Trauma and the Undoing of Character.* Simon and Schuster, 1995.

Sinek, Simon. *Start with Why: How Great Leaders Inspire Everyone to Take Action.* Portfolio, 2011.

Taylor, Teneal. *From Burnout to Balance: Work–Life Balance Strategies from a Single-Working Mom.* Independently published, 2025.

Tears for Fears. "Tears for Fears - Everybody Wants to Rule the World." *Tears For Fears,* August 9, 2013. Video, 4 min., 50 sec. https://youtu.be/aGCdLKXNF3w.

Turan, Kenneth. "Review: 'Gran Torino.'" *Los Angeles Times*, December 12, 2008. https://www.latimes.com/entertainment/la-et-torino12-2008dec12-story.html.

Turletti, Pablo. "Sustainability and Profitability: Why They Can and Should Go Hand in Hand. *Forbes,* May 20, 2022. https://www.forbes.com/councils/forbescommunicationscouncil/2022/05/20/sustainability-and-profitability-why-they-can-and-should-go-hand-in-hand/.

Twain, Shania. *From This Moment On.* Atria Books, 2012.

U2. "I Still Haven't Found What I'm Looking For." *The Joshua Tree.* Island Records. Released March 9, 1987.

Verzuh, E. (2021). *The Fast Forward MBA in Project Management: The Comprehensive, Easy-to-Read Handbook for Beginners and Pros.* 6th ed. Wiley, 2021.

Walt Disney Company. "The Walt Disney Company partners with U.S. State Department on 'Hidden No More' Exchange Program." October 28, 2019. https://thewaltdisneycompany.com/the-walt-disney-company-partners-with-u-s-state-department-on-hidden-no-more-exchange-program/.

Warren, Michael John, dir. *7 Days Out*. Season 1, episode 2, "Eleven Madison Park." Released December 21, 2018, on Netflix.

Warren, Rick. *The Purpose Driven Life: What on Earth Am I Here For?* Zondervan, 2002.

Whedon, Joss, dir. *Avengers: Age of Ultron*. Marvel Studios, 2015.

Wiersbe, W. W. *On Being a Leader for God*. Grand Rapids, MI: Baker Books, 2011.

Wilde, Oscar. "The Decay of Lying: An Observation." In *Intentions*. James R. Osgood, McIlvaine & Co., 1889.

Wood Hills, Katy. "CA Students Visit Monet Exhibit, Learn from His Struggles." *Colorado Academy News*, January 29, 2020. https://www.coloradoacademy.org/news/news-details/~board/ca-news/post/ca-students-visit-monet-exhibit-learn-from-his-struggles.

Illustration Credits

Front Cover

- 5-Stars: Viewvear.5-stars.

Preface

- Balancing scale. Rank Sol. *Balance scale.*

GPS Navigator

- Tool box. vectoricons344. *Tool pouch.*

Chapter 1 – Personality (Identity). Flat Vectors. *Male car driver.*

- Shifting gear. Tatianapankova. *Manual transmission.*

Chapter 3 – Passion. Vectorstall. *Passion.*

Chapter 4 – Problem-solving. NhorPhai. *Business, partner, puzzle icon.*

- Mind Map. Jino. *Graph.*
- Flow Chart. Bernd Lakenbrink. *Flow chart.*
- The 5 Whys. Iconmakers. *Questions.*
- Ishikawa Diagram. Soapi. *Fishbone.*
- Design Thinking. vectoricons344. *Emotional Intelligence.*

Chapter 5. Plan. Designer's Circle. *Destination, location, mark icon.*

- Balancing scale. Tawny Whatmore. *Scales.*
- Film icon. trang5000. *Film.*
- Game controller. Valter Bispo. *Xbox.*
- Musical note. Shwepes. *Melody.*

Chapter 6 – Profit. Adrien Coquet. *Profit.*

- Leverage. Eko Purnomo. *Teamwork.*
- Emotional Intelligence. Pronto Illustration. *Heart hands.*
- Agility. AdbA Icons. *Flexible.*
- Direction. Vectors Point. *Compass.*
- Enterprising Skills. IconMark. *Route.*
- Responsibility. Abdul Latif. *Checklist.*
- Plan. Yuniarti Pahlevie. *Schedule.*
- Lead. syafii5758. *Leadership development.*
- Organize. nine. *Flow chart.*
- Monitor. Eldad Efata. *Magnifying glass.*

www.ingramcontent.com/pod-product-compliance
Lightning Source LLC
Chambersburg PA
CBHW061802120626
46550CB00005B/2097